CREATING AND PLANTING GARDEN TROUGHS

Joyce Fingerut
Rex Murfitt

B. B. MACKEY BOOKS
P. O. Box 475
Wayne, PA 19087

creating and planting garden troughs

Photographs by Jane Grushow

Varied uses and
treatments of
garden troughs.

Rex Murfitt

iii   Three photographs by Joyce Fingerut

CREATING AND PLANTING GARDEN TROUGHS

Published 1999 by B. B. Mackey Books, P. O. Box 475, Wayne, PA 19087. All rights
reserved. Information: bbmackey@prodigy.net

The cover photo, by Jane Grushow, shows an elegant line of troughs created and
planted by author Rex Murfitt at his home in British Columbia. The title page photo of
Saxifraga burseriana 'Minor' is by Rex Murfitt, as is the back cover photo of
Sempervivum arachnoideum in bloom.

ISBN 1-893443-00-0
Library of Congress Catalog Card Number **99-70366**

horticulture
container gardening
alpine gardening

Contents

Betty Mackey

Jane Grushow

Trough gardens created and grown in Pennsylvania by Nick Klise and Morris West.

Preface

Rex Murfitt

Stone agricultural troughs have been popular as horticultural ornaments for decades. They have been planted, photographed and exhibited, further extending their popularity.

Once the supply of original stone troughs dwindled, and labor costs made new stone troughs prohibitive, feasible methods for producing concrete looka-likes were developed. These methods were highly informal: the "formulas" developed in a casual fashion and reported anecdotally.

Over the years, articles appeared in horticultural journals and home and garden magazines, written from the vantage point of the home gardener or the home designer. Specialty plantsmen, especially rock gardeners, wrote in their bulletins to extoll the virtues of the trough as an ideal environment for alpines and other growing gems. Recipes for the cement-based, trough-making substance, dubbed "hypertufa," appeared with great frequency. The technique has varied although the basic ingredients of hypertufa have remained roughly the same.

New products from professionals who work with cement have recently become available to amateur builders, and horticultural magazine articles have duly reflected their arrival. But brief articles, no matter how clearly written, necessarily select and condense the information. Explanations of how hypertufa looks and feels at various stages of its manufacture are out, but assumptions that you have access to the materials and know how to use them are in. Plant lists contain little discussion of the plants offered.

It was clear to us that the information needed to be expanded and elaborated; questions raised and answered; experiences shared. Failures and problems had to be noted, as they are as much a part of the learning experience as success.

This is the basis of our book. Our *Introduction* takes you through a bit of history, recounting a few of the many anecdotes that cling to the story of the trough's metamorphosis from cattle feeder to coveted ornament. This is followed by a quick overview of the development of modern hypertufa. From this, the reader should understand that the recipe and techniques offered here represent only one approach to making troughs.

Chapter Two offers the clearest and most comprehensive set of instructions we can offer. There are explanations of all the ingredients, with details on how to find and buy them. For convenience, this part includes a one-page, photocopiable shopping checklist. This is followed by very basic, step-by-step guidelines for preparing and proceding to make strong, sound hypertufa troughs. Additionally we offer options for decorative troughs and decorative finishes, as well as other items which can be made with hypertufa, thus expanding the repertoire.

Logic dictates that the next step is planting the trough, and Chapter Three begins with the considerations for suitable sites in which to place a trough. The discussion moves on to the environment within the trough: soil, mulch, rocks or other accessories; all the paraphernalia necessary or desirable for the well-designed, well-planted trough.

And, of course, the plants! Chapter Four discusses the pleasures and problems of locating plants for your troughs: from studying them in their natural rocky habitats to acquiring them from specialty sources, as either plants or seeds. Tips and caveats for the frenzied plant collector are provided. A brief overview of botanical nomenclature is included, as well. Here we supply *Plant Talk: Recommended Plants for Troughs,* covering quite a range of plants with descriptions of their sizes, colors and various subtle differences, with clear explanations of their cultural requirements and best uses. Many of them are pictured. This rich variety of options will make your personal selection easier—or, perhaps, more difficult, but still fun!

The grand finale, Chapter Five, is a working plan for a generous assortment of trough plantings in a home setting. Measurements, recipes, plant lists (annotated, of course) and details abound to help make your first, or latest, attempts with troughs a success.

This book should be just a beginning: we expect that you will want to expand your learning and your experiences in this new skill, with its exciting horticultural possiblities. To make futher information easily accessible, we have added detailed listings for the *Sources and Resources* section, plus an index of plants and a general index, to provide all the information you will need in order to create wonderful trough gardens.

The ingredients, proportions and methods presented in this book are based upon the experiences of Joyce Fingerut in making troughs and giving trough-making workshops and demonstrations. The lists and descriptions of plants considered suitable for life in a trough are the result of Rex Murfitt's decades of wide experience in growing, propagating and contemplating plants, both in and out of garden troughs.

A word of warning: although building troughs is an exciting and creative process, it can also be a messy project, with some potential dangers and pitfalls. Common sense belongs high on the list of things to bring to the workplace. Working with equipment or chemicals means keeping your wits about you; the bits of safety advice scattered throughout the book can help keep you focussed. And, although we offer you our best advice and wish you the best possible results, there can be no guarantees: the best craftsmen make mistakes; the best plantsmen lose plants.

While the authors have each shared information from their specific areas of expertise, this book is the better and richer for all of the contributions from their friends.

Photographer Jane Grushow was instrumental in bringing all parties together: Joyce and Rex as authors with Betty as editor/publisher. She was the "official" recorder at all the messy workshops, and has chased photos far afield.

Michael and Jan Slater provided help in all ways: work sessions for making troughs, on-call answers to questions regarding everything from plants to rocks. Readers will also enjoy following the progression of one of Mike's troughs: from turkey-platter form to Flower Show winner.

Roberta Berg opened her home and garden to Joyce for a day's photo session among her artistic creations and adaptations of the trough-maker's craft. She is also willing to share her insights and skills with others, and can be contacted to give presentations to interested groups (see *Sources and Resources*).

Many thanks to Ron McBeath, who, while he was a curator at the Royal Botanic Garden, Edinburgh, generously allowed Joyce free access to the troughs and ample time, outside of public hours, to photograph them.

Lawrence Thomas and Harold McBride are generous friends who volunteered to lend slides of their own efforts, which helped to illuminate some of the finer points of planting and maintaining troughs.

Reginald Gifford, owner of Michael's Nook (Grasmere, England) was kind enough to share his knowledge and the fine private collection of troughs after it had been reported that a guest (Joyce) was creeping around his many troughs at the inn, on all fours, taking endless photos.

Joyce and Rex wish to acknowledge Betty Mackey's personal generosity and flexible work policies throughout the entire process of publication.

Anne Freeman

Trough collection at Wave Hill in Bronx, New York

Jane Grushow

HYPERTUFA

Before we can talk about hypertufa, we should have an idea of what tufa is and its role in trough gardening.

Back in the early 1930's, it was discovered that some alpine plants grew exceptionally well in a substance called tufa rock. Tufa is a soft, porous calcareous rock and is formed when water containing carbon-dioxide seeps through limestone formations. Through natural biochemical reactions, cooling of the water and evaporation, the dissolved limestone finally precipitates out as a solid calcium-carbonate substance. It forms around odds and ends of debris and decayed matter, which eventually rot away, leaving numerous tiny tunnels and other air spaces within the rock. Tufa's color varies in shades of off-white, from light gray to yellow-gray. It is also variable in its hardness: it is softest and most workable as it comes out of the ground and hardens with continued exposure to the air.

Jane Grushow

Natural tufa planted with alpines.

Tufa deposits exist in many places throughout the world, including many sites in the British Isles and North America. Alpine gardeners soon discovered the natural affinity between this lime rock, with its perfect drainage, and some of the more difficult alpine plants. Its attractive appearance and relatively light weight also made it popular. It was soon discovered that supplies were not all that plentiful, and it has since become a rather scarce and expensive commodity. This problem, coupled with the cost of transporting the stuff, sparked a few gardeners to seek an inexpensive and accessible alternative.

One man came up with the idea of mixing peat moss into concrete: his original idea being to produce a lightweight, porous substance for reproducing tufa stones. He poured a creamy mixture of concrete and peatmoss into a wet sand mold, where real rocks had been used as patterns. A quote from one of the early experimenters shows an interesting insight into the rock gardeners of the 1930's: "Much heart searching by purists at the thought of using introduced artificiality into the rock garden."

It was not long before enterprising gardeners discovered that this product, now dubbed "hypertufa," was an excellent material for casting replicas of the coveted stone troughs. In light of today's advances, it is fun to look at one of the early recipes (measured by bulk): one part sand; two parts peatmoss, and one part Portland cement.

Once hypertufa began to be used by gardeners, like any other recipe passed from one set of creative hands to another, it was modified to suit the needs and tastes of the gardener. The proportions were varied, often using additional cement for increased strength (although this can reach a point of diminishing returns). And while this Portland cement base has not changed over the intervening decades, and peat is still added, there have been many other changes, notably in substitutes for previously used ingredients. First, in the interest of creating a more

5

lightweight substance, the sand was replaced by perlite. For added durability and long-term strength, the cast troughs were reinforced with chickenwire.

This procedure was as time consuming as it was unpleasant, requiring some effort, skill and not a little patience. It has been with great relief that the new synthetic fibers for reinforcing concrete have been recently substituted. Fibers of some sort had always been used in even the earliest manufacture of concrete; these were natural fibers of jute, straw and horsehair. The new synthetic multi-filament fibers are made of nylon, acrylic or polypropylene. They have been incorporated into the latest recipes for hypertufa. And for increased durability, liquid acrylic is also used in place of some of the water, making the finished troughs more impermeable to water—reducing the effects of freezing and thawing.

More recently, our understanding of the role of water in this process has improved. Previously, the consistency of the hypertufa mix was not an issue, it was supposed to be loose and workable. Now, we know that the drier the hyper-tufa mixture, the stronger the resulting trough, so instructions have been modified to reflect this. Forms and molds for troughs have been at the same time simplified and strengthened, over the previously used wood forms or cardboard boxes. The range of possible alternative forms and shapes now runs to the infinite. The new color additives and finishes offer new ways of either making the hypertufa look more nearly like stone or expressing artistic individuality.

There are, obviously, many other ways to create and plant trough gardens. If you have found a mix or a method that works well for you, there is no reason to change. However, by reading this book and studying the methods presented, you may come to have a clearer understanding of the processes at work. The discussions of plants and planting options may offer a few new ideas, so that you just might be tempted to try some new projects.

And that is the whole idea!

Saxifraga moschata 'Cloth of Gold'.

Chapter Two
Constructing a Hypertufa Trough

Rex Murfitt

It is possible to make your own troughs, working alone or in a group, without actually quarrying and chiseling solid rock. Here are step-by-step directions for building attractive, long-lasting, weatherproof hypertufa troughs from the ground up, perfectly suited to your designs and requirements.

The best material for forming troughs is **hypertufa,** a cement-based product. Classified as a lightweight-aggregate concrete, it is a sturdy material that can be molded, colored, and textured to resemble any natural stone from porous tufa to solid granite.

You could use standard concrete, but it is impossibly heavy, around 150 pounds per cubic foot. Hypertufa weighs only a fraction of that. At a relatively light 20 to 50 pounds per cubic foot, its weight is almost entirely due to the cement, not the "featherweight" aggregates.

Hypertufa is also easily workable. At the proper stage in its curing, you can add textural interest and character to the surface of the planter. It is also porous enough to allow the surface to hold moisture for those mosses and lichens that add character and give the appearance of age. Hypertufa's natural porosity also provides some thermal insulation. Although not as durable as concrete, it has been proven to hold together for a decade and more, which is more than can be said for many of the contained plants. Good drainage will aid longevity, as there will be less water retained to freeze and thaw, contract and expand, damaging both container and plants.

7

GETTING IT TOGETHER

Be forewarned: making troughs is very nearly like work. It takes thought and preparation beforehand and energy during the process. Prepare by having everything on site and at hand before beginning the construction of the trough. Working with cement-based products is very time sensitive, and you cannot stop in the middle of working in order to go off in search of a misplaced tool, let alone to buy a forgotten ingredient. It may take a while to assemble and organize all the tools and arrange the workplace, so be sure to allow enough time to do it in several steps.

Each hypertufa ingredient has a specific role, chemically or mechanically. Please read carefully about them all and resolve any questions and shopping issues ahead of time. Assemble hypertufa ingredients and other trough-making paraphernalia in a clean site: one that is spacious, well-lit, well-ventilated, and heated to the point where you can work comfortably.

LET'S GO SHOPPING: Hypertufa Ingredients
Cement

The most basic component of hypertufa is *cement.* Pure cement should never be confused with *concrete,* which is the finished product: a mixture of cement plus aggregates. In concrete, the aggregates are sand and stone, which each weigh about 100 pounds per cubic foot. It is the aggregates that are the key to the difference in weight between concrete and hypertufa. When making hypertufa, sand and stone are replaced by peat and perlite, which are negligible in weight (an average of about five pounds per cubic foot). The trickiest part in making durable hypertufa is understanding the nature and the role of the cement.

Portland cement is a kind of cement, not a brand name. It was given this name, in the early nineteenth century, by its English discoverer, Joseph Aspdin,

Jane Grushow

HYPERTUFA SHOPPING CHECKLIST

Supplies for making hypertufa mixture

- ❑ Type II Portland cement (not concrete mix)
- ❑ Perlite
- ❑ Peat
- ❑ Synthetic reinforcement fibers
- ❑ Cement colors
- ❑ Liquid acrylic bonding agent (non-rewettable type)
- ❑ Water supply and hose with shut-off nozzle
- ❑ Spray bottle
- ❑ Mixing container (mortar pan or wheelbarrow)
- ❑ Measuring container
- ❑ Hoe, shovel, trowel, etc.
- ❑ Scoop (optional)
- ❑ 5-gallon bucket (optional)

Safety

- ❑ STURDY RUBBER GLOVES— an absolute necessity!
- ❑ Dust mask
- ❑ Protective goggles

Supplies for making rectangular trough forms

- ❑ Foam insulation boards
- ❑ Knife
- ❑ Yardstick
- ❑ Pencil, pen or marker
- ❑ Nails
- ❑ Duct tape (what can we do without it?)
- ❑ Forms for drainage holes
- ❑ Hardware cloth
- ❑ Landscape fabric

Equipment for shaping other troughs

- ❑ Oval baking pans (heavy agate pans, not disposable aluminum)
- ❑ Pressed peat hanging-basket liners
- ❑ Containers (bonsai, bulb pans, Styrofoam™ boxes, etc.)
- ❑ Plastic bins and other household containers
- ❑ Packed, moist sand for free-form molds or for modifying shapes of other molds

Tools for finishing and texturing

- ❑ Sturdy household utensils, with dull blades, that are past home use
- ❑ Broad knife, screwdriver, asparagus fork, putty knife or pull-type paint scraper
- ❑ Wire brush
- ❑ Whisk broom
- ❑ Surface stains or paints (optional)
- ❑ Hand-held propane torch

General supplies

- ❑ Sturdy wooden board, slightly larger than the planned trough, for moving it before it dries
- ❑ Plastic sheeting
- ❑ Scissors
- ❑ Sieve (optional)
- ❑ Large container to hold sieved peat
- ❑ Medium container to hold fluffed-up reinforcement fibers
- ❑ Tables (optional; it may be easier to work on the ground)
- ❑ Knee pads (optional, for people working on the ground)

who felt that the product looked and worked very much like a type of natural stone quarried from the Isle of Portland, off the southern coast of Dorset. Type I Portland cement is the type most widely available, and it is used for almost all smaller projects—small, that is, by comparison with massive buildings or bridge abutments. Cements other than Type I Portland are also available for specialized uses. Masonry concrete is Portland cement plus lime and an air-entraining agent to make the masonry cement more easily workable. The remaining types, II through V, address special problems in construction, such as a sulfate hazard or situations where the heat-producing reaction of curing can cause a problem.

Portland cement is generally offered in basic gray, but is also available as white cement and, occasionally, with various tints. White cement contains very little (less than 0.3 percent) iron oxide and manganese oxide, is free of other impurities and must be processed by different methods in special oil- or gas-burning mills. This all adds to the cost of white cement, which is an unnecessary expense unless you are planning on making a pastel-colored trough. When white cement is used as the base for hypertufa, it can give a bright, unnatural glow to pigments added for coloring. Under certain light, it can turn a trough that originally seemed to be the color of red shale stone into a shimmering flamingo pink! So, wait until you have experimented and are certain that you really need it, before choosing it.

Portland cement is purchased in 94-pound paper sacks. This amount equals about one cubic yard of finished cement. Now, although I have been urging you to have all materials ready at the site, the cement should not be purchased too far ahead of time, as it can absorb ambient moisture and harden before it is used. If it must be kept for a long time, wrap it in plastic and store it in a dry area where the temperature remains constant. Never buy or use cement which has lumps or is not free-flowing.

Aggregates

The aggregates used in both concrete and hypertufa are basically inert. They do not react with the water or each other, but provide a base to which the cement paste adheres. They can form anywhere from two-thirds to three-fourths of the volume of the finished product, so their own weight is an important factor. In concrete, it is the heavy aggregates (sand or stone) which contribute to the durability of construction projects.

Aggregates should be well graded in size, from coarse to fine. In concrete, this means gravel down to sand, and in hypertufa, perlite to peat. This grading will result in a range of particle sizes, so that there is one the right size to fill each void, making the mix denser and stronger. The cement and water form a paste which bonds all particles together, once it has cured.

Strength is related to the proportion of cement in the mix. If the strongest, most durable container is needed, then the classic concrete mixture, rather than hypertufa, should be used. If weight is a factor but *some* additional strength is required, use a somewhat higher proportion of cement in the hypertufa mixture. In the garden, it is not necessary to build for the ages, so some longevity can be sacrificed in the interest of portability.

Perlite is a silica derivative, and a good lightweight substitute for sand as an aggregate. It is a volcanic, glassy material that has been ground and then superheated to 1400 degrees F. This makes minute amounts of water contained within each particle suddenly expand, just like popcorn popping, puffing the glassy bits into a spongy, lightweight material. Perlite weighs only 5 to 8 pounds per cubic foot, compared to 100 pounds for sand. Used not only in gardens, perlite is also an aggregate approved for heavy construction by the American Society for Testing Materials (ASTM).

Use a *dust mask* when working around perlite from the moment that you first open the bag, as great clouds of irritating dust are given off when measuring and handling it.

Peat can be bought dry or slightly moistened, but should never be entirely wet. It serves very well as the finer aggregate, filling the voids between the larger particles of perlite.

The bonding of cement with lightweight aggregates is at least as good as with sand and gravel, the usual aggregates. The bond may even be better due to the rough surface and porosity of the perlite, which allows penetration of cement paste into the particles.

There will be no serious loss of durability from using lightweight aggregates unless the trough becomes saturated and is subjected to freezing and thawing before curing is complete. Problems can be avoided if:

1) the hypertufa mixture has been made as impenetrable as possible by careful compaction in the molds; and

2) the hypertufa has had sufficient time to cure and dry before it is subjected to freezing.

It is wise to make the troughs at least a month before the projected first frosts in fall, or to store the curing troughs in a frost-free place such as a basement or garage.

The New Fibers

Synthetic reinforcing fibers are now used in the building industry to help control shrinkage and cracking in concrete. They work by keeping the separate microscopic pores that form as cement hardens from joining and forming larger cracks. If allowed to enlarge, cracks threaten the strength and life of the concrete. Fibers are the modern replacement for wire reinforcement and, for a garden ornament, are all the reinforcement needed.

Chickenwire was previously used for reinforcement in the garden trough, but it was unwieldy, and the resulting trough needed thick walls to hide the wires. Fiber reinforcement allows for lighter troughs with thinner walls plus more freedom in design. There are numerous types of fibers used: natural (such as wood, sisal, coconut, bamboo, jute), steel, glass and

Jane Grushow

plastics.The fibers we use are a type of plastic, not fiberglass, and so will not leave any invisible, irritating shards in your fingers. They can be handled with bare hands, and will need to be greatly handled: the fibers must be separated and "fluffed" before incorporating them into the hypertufa mix.

Fibers are sold by a number of companies in a variety of lengths, colors, and thicknesses. Your best choice would be concrete gray, not white (unless you are working with white cement); and short (about 3/4 inch), rather than long.

Each bag of fibers is pre-measured to provide enough for one cubic yard of mixture, the amount made from one 94-pound bag of cement. Fibers can be added at any stage of the mixing process, but it is easier to incorporate them after dry ingredients have been slightly moistened. Industry standards recommend that the fibers be mixed into the cement and aggregates for five to ten minutes. Some brands have a special coating to enhance even dispersal.

Liquid Acrylic

Liquid acrylic bonding agent has lately been recommended as part of the hypertufa mix. When used as an integral part of a mortar or concrete mixture, it increases resistance to impact, abrasion, water absorption (thus improving dura-bility·through many more freeze-thaw cycles), chemicals, ultraviolet light, and heat. It can be used either as part of the hypertufa mixture, or as a surface preparation to increase adhesion when patching a crack or "plastering" hypertufa over an object such as a styrofoam container.

Because the acrylic is in liquid form, it will replace some of the water, usually in proportions of 1:3 (acrylic:water). It is recommended that no more than half of the water be replaced by the acrylic (a 1:1 solution). This can present certain difficulties when trying to estimate in advance how much acrylic will ultimately be needed, since the amount of water needed depends on many factors, and the final amount is arrived at by guess and feel. However, like a good cook, the trough maker will soon learn to work by intuition. And no real harm can come of using either too much, or too little, of the acrylic in a trough. Let's keep things in perspective—we're not constructing the World Trade Center here!

There are several brands of liquid acrylic. Whichever you choose, read all information and cautions on the label carefully.

Colors

Coloring can either be added into the hypertufa as it is mixed, or applied to the surface of a finished trough. Cement colors, available as *ground pigments*, are added to the hypertufa mixture. You can closely match the color of your local stone for a more natural effect. These colors are made from oxides of iron and other minerals or extracted from reclaimed metals. There are also synthetic oxides, which extend the range of colors and offer deeper tints. We are talking about natural, ground mineral colors, not the artificial blues and greens of the swimming pool trade.

The pigments are finely ground to disperse easily and evenly throughout the cement mixture. They physically bind with grains of cement. Because it is not an inexpensive item, use only as much coloring as necessary—perhaps about a cupful for each batch of hypertufa. The colors are sold by bulk (which is less

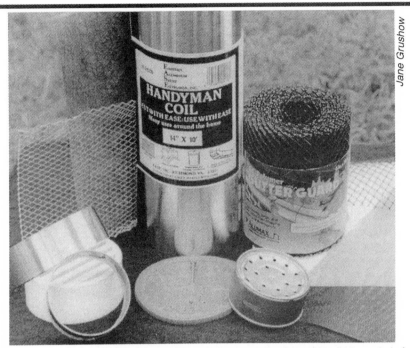

Drainage holes must be adequate in size. Here are some supplies for making drainage hole forms, plus mesh and landscape fabrics to lay over them in order to hold soil in and keeps bugs out.

the surface of the foamboard prior to snapping off the piece. If you will be using the knife for the entire cut, find one with a sharp (or resharpenable) blade, plain or serrated, that is eight to ten inches long—long enough for a sawing motion.

Nails should have a good-sized head, and be three inches long, if working with foam insulation board that has a thickness of one and a half inches; four-inch nails are needed for two-inch thick boards.

Duct tape is all you need for bracing the exterior of the foamboard form. I can't believe you don't already have a roll or two around the house.

The *forms for drainage holes* in the floor of the trough can be made from anything sturdy and straight-sided. Best of all are pre-molded PVC drain covers, which come in a range of diameters; check plumbing supplies at the hardware store. Or use a tuna can with the top and bottom removed, a slice of PVC pipe at least two inches in diameter, or a strip of metal flashing rolled into a circle and held with (what else?) duct tape. Cover the raw edges of metal flashing with tape, to protect fingers from nasty cuts.

Like the walls of the trough form, drainage hole forms must be sturdy, in order to hold an opening in the floor of the trough while you are pounding in cement all around it. The drainage hole form should be as thick as the trough floor, which is usually two inches or more. I prefer using forms while constructing the troughs to making holes afterward in the wet or cured hypertufa.

Wooden dowels are also suggested for making drainage holes, but they are skimpy in size when compared to the area for which they must provide drainage. Being so small, they can clog easily, and soon provide no drainage at all.

Hardware cloth, which is not cloth at all but a wire grid or screen with half-inch openings, will sit on top of the drainage hole. It can be cemented in

17

Jane Grushow

A trough, unwrapped after its initial curing,
with tools used for texturing its walls.

place as the bottom of the trough is being made, or simply placed in the trough at the time of planting. This will not be necessary if you use the PVC drain cover, which has a grid already molded into its top.

Hardware cloth provides support for the next item: *landscape fabric*, which is a woven or felted textile, usually in basic black. This loose fabric should sit atop the rigid hardware cloth (which is over the drainage hole) in order to prevent the planting medium from washing out of the trough, and keep some bugs from crawling in. Suitable substitutes are Reemay™ fabric or plastic or metal screening material—anything that is water permeable and easily cut with scissors.

Finishing tools are used after the initial curing, when the trough has hardened enough to hold together, but is still incompletely consolidated. At this stage, hypertufa can be scratched and gouged by any sturdy instrument that can leave its mark. Stiff putty knives can do the job, as can asparagus forks, kitchen knives with inflexible blades (like butter knives), screwdrivers, wire brushes or anything else with a solid blade and a sturdy handle. When working a trough that is built over an inverted form, so that the exterior wall of the trough is exposed, you can do some of the texturing while the hypertufa is still wet, with a stiff whisk broom or an imprinting tool.

There are many options for finishing and ornamenting a trough. Textures can be achieved by either adding onto or carving into the surface. Exterior colors can be applied to a wet surface or to a partially hardened one. Use stains for transparent tinting, solid colors for deeper shades.

You can see how all these details should be thought through before any work can begin! Be sure to read pages 35 to 48 for more suggestions and options.

The final job in finishing the trough, before planting is even considered, will be the removal of any visible traces of the reinforcing fibers protruding from the surface. This job is easily done with a hand-held *propane torch,* which you can find at hardware stores in the section where plumbing supplies are sold.

Work Area

General supplies include enough *plastic sheeting* to protect the area where you will be working (if necessary) and also sheets to completely enclose each of the troughs. A good strong plastic, of 2 to 3 mil thickness, is commonly sold by the roll. Widths of five or ten feet (folded down to no more than a yard wide), and lengths of 20, 50, or 100 feet are available. The plastic can be cleaned and reused many times. *Scissors* will cut it easily, so keep a pair at hand, for this and for cutting duct tape and other odds and ends.

If you will not be leaving the troughs in place to cure, but will be moving them to another, more suitable area, then you will need a *sturdy board or tray* beneath each trough. This board should be at least 4 inches (ideally 6 to 8 inches) larger than the outside perimeter of the form or mold. It must be sturdy enough to support the weight of several pounds of wet hypertufa. A piece of exterior grade plywood is ideal; a leftover piece of 2-inch thick foam board can serve nicely for the smaller troughs.

The troughs may be made directly on the ground, which many people find to be the most comfortable position. This brings everything beneath you, so that you can get your whole body's weight to bear on it for best compaction (or, to use the proper concrete-making term, consolidation). Use a *rubber kneeling pad* for comfort, or even a rectangle of the foam insulation board under your knees. If kneeling while you work is not appealing or comfortable, then the trough can be made on a table. Any *tables* you use must be sturdy enough to be pounded upon, with the tabletop below waist height.

A *sieve* for the peat is nice, but optional. You can simply break up the clumps of peat with your fingers, removing stray sticks and other substances.

You will need a *large container* to hold the refined peat. Because peat is a major component of hypertufa, be sure to have a container that will accommodate all of the peat needed by everyone involved.

You will also need a *smaller container* for the fibers. Use one with a wide opening so that the fibers can be repeatedly fluffed right in the container.

Time and Place

Time is not on the shopping checklist, but is usually at a premium. The first two stages of completing a trough require one session each, a day or two apart: the first to make the trough, and the second (after the initial curing) to finish and texture it.

The forms can be made ahead of time and stored until needed. Allow about three hours for the first session, once all the materials and ingredients have been assembled, and about half that for the finishing.

Timing is equally important: the trough will not be immediately ready for planting; it will need to cure for a month. Even then, additional time is helpful if you want to be certain that any excess free lime has leached away through the slow weathering process.

In most of the United States and Canada, a good time to work is late in summer. This allows for early fall planting, if you live in a climate with a long mild autumn—one long enough to allow time for the plants to settle in before the winter frosts. Late August is generally a slack season, horticulturally speaking, and the moist, warm air is conducive to rapid curing of hypertufa. The only caveat is to keep the trough from overheating, as curing is adversely affected by temperatures over 85 degrees F.

The best time to make a trough, if you are not too busy with cleanup and late planting chores, is during the fall. The mellow days of early autumn are perfect for such projects; and there will still be enough mild weather for proper curing of the trough. It can be stored inside the basement or garage, or sit outside, exposed to the elements over the winter, and will be ready for planting with the first frenzy of spring gardening.

Early spring can also be a good time. You will need either a day warm enough to work outside (in which case you would probably rather be gardening), or a suitable space to work indoors. If you construct the trough in March or early April, it will be ready for planting by May. If you begin much later, the weather may turn hot, and this is not kind to newly planted containers.

The *workplace* must offer all the proper conditions, for your own comfort as well as the requirements of the materials. Think ahead, as you are reading this, for likely work sites. The area, which can be indoors or out, must be well ventilated, because of all the dust raised by cement and perlite. Good lighting is necessary, as is elbow-room for everyone who will be mixing hypertufa and building troughs. If you will use a cement mixer, allow further space. If it is gasoline-powered, extra ventilation is a must, to diffuse and expel exhaust fumes. If it is an electric model, a nearby outlet is needed. An extension cord can be used only if it is heavy-duty, waterproof, and rated for exterior use.

The water source should be close at hand, whether using a hose or pre-filled sprinkling cans.

You can make troughs directly on the ground or on top of a sturdy table.

Cement and hypertufa can be worked at any temperature that is also comfortable for you. However, their ultimate strength is reduced by temperatures at either extreme. While heat speeds the setting of hypertufa, tests have shown that with an increase in temperature, there is a decrease in strength. Cold temperatures, below 50 degrees F, also compromise strength. Standard room temperatures, during the periods of working and curing of hypertufa, are best—the optimum temperature being a very comfortable 68 degrees F. If you are planning to work during a very warm or windy day, it will be best to work where you are sheltered from both sun and wind, to prevent the mixture from drying out to the point where it is too stiff to work.

Design and Planning

Think ahead and plan exactly what you want to make. First consider why you want to make a trough or troughs. Then plan a size, shape and finish to suit the needs of the plants, your site, and any design considerations (in that order!).

If you are making a hypertufa trough for the first time, it is best to begin with the simplest form, to get used to the method and the materials. Making a small, square trough will give you a sense of the process and timing, and the feel of the hypertufa mixture.

If you have worked with hypertufa in the past, even with older methods, you probably already have some firm ideas about what you want to do next. Still, you

If you will be moving the trough while it is still wet (to allow it to cure in a more out-of-the-way spot, or in the shade), now is the time to position the supporting board *beneath* the plastic.

Place the trough form directly on top of the plastic sheet. In the center of the trough form, on the plastic sheet, place one of the drainage hole forms (or two or more spaced along the bottom of a larger trough).

Have the piece of hardware cloth at hand, if you will be cementing it into place; the landscape fabric or screening will not be used until the trough is ready to be planted.

Once the forms have been assembled, begin to mix the hypertufa.

PREPARING THE INGREDIENTS

If you will be working alone, doing everything yourself, prepare each of the ingredients beforehand. You can even combine some of the ingredients, up to a point, if you find it more convenient to work in several shorter sessions, rather than one long workday.

When working in a group, divide the chores so that some members are cutting pieces of foam board for all of the forms, while others prepare the ingredients of the hypertufa mixture. Everyone, however, should have the opportunity to assemble his or her own form. It's a good learning experience.

Place the bag of *cement* on high, dry ground, well away from the area where the hose or any runoff from mixing might wet its contents. A bench or tabletop will keep it above the water line, while giving you easy access without bending. Cut an opening in the top (or the side, if the bag is lain horizontally); open it wide enough to allow both of your hands to maneuver the measuring container.

Sieve the *peat,* or at least break up all lumps and remove solid stems and twigs. Do enough for all the troughs to be made in this session. Store the prepared peat in an accessible container or plastic bag. The peat can be dry or slightly moistened, but never wet. By the way, those rejected chunky pieces are wonderful amendments for your garden soil.

Perlite needs no special preparation, but is very dusty, so use a dust mask when handling and measuring it. Mist it slightly to keep the dust down.

The *coloring* for the hypertufa, if any, should be on hand. Whatever type you use, read the instructions. If the color is to be integral, that is, a part of the hypertufa mix, add it when combining all the other ingredients. If it is surface coloring (stain, dry-shake hardener or paint), use it later in the finishing process.

For integral color admixtures, remember that a small amount goes a long way, especially when you consider that hypertufa need only be tinted, not deeply colored, in order to look natural.

Try out dry colors at about one cup per batch (a batch varies but often half fills a wheelbarrow), to see whether the depth of color is what you had in mind. Also remember that the true color cannot be judged until the trough has finished its final curing, one month after its construction, and will probably turn out to be lighter than you had thought.

The fibers—ah, the Sisyphean task of fluffing the fibers. Pulling and keeping the clumps of fibers apart into single fibers is as difficult as it is necessary. Do and redo this as much as your sanity can tolerate. But be forewarned: they will reclump when your back is turned! Extra time spent at mixing the wet hypertufa mixture, once the fibers have been added, will compensate somewhat for this clumping tendency and will disperse the fibers more evenly through the mix.

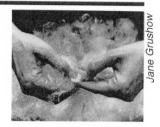

Jane Grushow

MAKING HYPERTUFA

The basic recipe for hypertufa was developed from the classic recipe for mortar: one part cement to three parts aggregates. Mortar and hypertufa are proportionately higher in cement than concrete and are, therefore, stronger. In mortar, the aggregates are heavy sand and stone. Hypertufa, with its lighter aggregates, peat and perlite, makes a trough with one-fourth the weight, while giving up very little strength and durability. If you are concerned about the container's longevity (beyond a decade or two) and not primarily its weight, then use the heavier aggregates. The proportions and procedures are the same.

Measure by volume. The size of the measuring unit is not crucial, but the same unit must be used for the three main ingredients: cement, peat and perlite. You will measure one part of cement for every three parts of aggregate. Since peat and perlite together form the aggregate, they should, in combination, form three-quarters of the final volume. In numerical terms, you can measure either:

1 part cement		3 parts cement
1-1/2 parts peat	or:	4 parts peat
1-1/2 parts perlite		5 parts perlite

The remaining ingredients are added as needed or to your preference, and will soon be discussed more fully.

Begin with Dry Ingredients

Put on your rubber gloves, then the dust mask and safety goggles.

Measure the dry ingredients and combine them in the mortar pan or wheelbarrow. Start with the cement, then add the aggregates and, if using them, the dry color pigments. It is preferable to work in smaller batches, using up one batch while it is still properly moistened and workable, before making the next batch. The fibers, though dry, are added with the wet ingredients.

When making a small batch, you can pour the entire amount of each ingredient required for the batch into the mixing container. But, if you will be making a larger batch, add the ingredients, one-half or one-third at a time, in several layers, in order to save some of the shoveling required to mix all the ingredients completely. Then, using a shovel (to lift and turn) or a hoe (to push and pull, which is easier on the back), or even large trowels or scoops, mix everything together completely and thoroughly. Working *from the outside into the center,* turn the material in the pile over and over (and over!) until the entire pile of dry ingredients is uniform in color and texture.

In the same way that a cooking recipe will occasionally say, "can be made to this point and finished the next day," the dry ingredients can be combined in one session, with the remaining work to be completed at another time. This is helpful if you have limited time for each work session. Also, by doing this, you can make up one large batch of dry ingredients ahead of time, to be used for completing several small projects later. But be certain to store the dry cement mixture in a container that is absolutely moistureproof, not merely waterproof.

When the time comes to complete the project, move on to the next steps. However, before wetting the mixture, it would be a good idea to remove and store a small portion of the already-mixed dry ingredients. If you accidentally add too much water (and it happens more often than not), you will have dry mix on hand, in the correct proportions, to bring the hypertufa mixture back into balance.

Water Makes it Happen

You will need enough water to be certain that all cement particles come into contact with water. This will form a strong cement paste, which will bond with the aggregates. However, too much water will upset the optimal water/cement ratio, resulting in a diluted mix and a weaker product, even after all of the curing and drying processes have been completed. The foremost factor in the strength of hypertufa is the proportion of water to cement.

There is an optimal amount of water to be used: the amount that is needed to hydrate all the particles of cement—and no more! Any excess water will leave behind more pores as it dries, compromising strength and watertightness. The pores eventually join and expand to become cracks. The cracks will retain water from rain or from watering the plants, which will freeze and thaw during the winter. This further expands cracks and can weaken parts of the structure, which may crumble and break away.

This may not always present a problem, and is not always an undesirable result aesthetically, but it should occur only by choice. Some gardeners prefer a more porous hypertufa for its rugged look, the freer drainage, how it lends itself to a free-form shape, and the way it crumbles into a look of refined antiquity, so they are willing to forego durability. Use the correct amount of water needed for the desired result. By doubling the amount of water, you could lose up to half of the trough's strength.

Iron or organic matter in the mixing/curing water may cause staining, which can either be avoided or used to create a desired effect. Iron oxides are sometimes used for a decorative stain, which is applied to the surface of the cured trough.

The pH of the water should be about 6.0 to 8.0; water that is too acid could adversely affect the hardening of the cement product. Water containing high levels of chloride (such as water from a swimming pool), sulfates or salts (from ocean or salt-marsh) or organic particles will also lessen the strength of the hypertufa.

Professionals working with structural concrete find that the optimal amount of water for durability produces a mixture that is too stiff for construction purposes: too dry to be easily poured into a mold. A looser, wetter mixture handles more easily. This is why some magazine articles have recommended a hypertufa mixture that resembles "sloppy cottage cheese." This looser mixture may be easier to mold, but does not lead to a long-lived trough. Fortunately, when hypertufa is being packed into molds and forms by hand, you can work with a stiffer mixture. Therefore, you are in a position to manufacture the strongest possible hypertufa.

The true hardening process occurs, not during the period of drying out after mixing, but during hydration, a chemical process in which water and cement particles interact. This is why concrete is able to harden underwater (using hydraulic cement), as well as on land. The strongest concrete/hypertufa results when every particle of cement has become hydrated; that is, come into contact with the water. To do this, the mixture must be kept continually moist during the mixing, packing and long curing processes. This is why the process is called curing, and not drying.

Moistening the Cement

If you will be adding a liquid acrylic (which I heartily recommend), add it at this point. If you have worked before with hypertufa, and have established exactly (more or less) how much water will eventually go into the mix, then you can pre-mix the acrylic with the water. The recommended dilution is about one part acrylic to three parts water. The proportion of acrylic can be increased, where extra adhesion is an issue, as in repairs or skim-coating an existing container with hypertufa; but never replace more than half the water with the liquid acrylic. If you are working by "guestimate," then add a cup or two of acrylic, drizzling it evenly over the dry ingredients.

To begin the transformation of your pile of grayish dry particles into hypertufa, make an indentation in the center, add some water, and then continue to turn the dry ingredients into the wet center until the water is uniformly distributed.

At this point, add the fluffed-out fibers, scattering them evenly over the surface of the mixture. How much of the fibers? I hate to say this, but: it depends. Consider the size of your batch and extrapolate, based on the directions given by the manufacturers: "one pound-and-a-half package for one 94-pound bag of cement." In general terms, a generous handful of fluffy fibers will probably do it: too much is certainly not a problem and, for a garden ornament, too little will not precipitate a crisis, either.

Continue turning and mixing, turning and mixing, until the fibers seem fairly well dispersed. You will continue to see occasional clumps and tufts, but the majority of fibers will have spread evenly throughout the mixture. As the ingredients are being mixed, additional water can be added, if needed.

Now, how can you tell if more water is needed? By using the same test that you often use to see whether garden soil is too wet to be worked. Wearing the sturdy rubber gloves, take a handful of the hypertufa mixture and squeeze. When you open your hand, the clump of hypertufa should be moist enough to hold together, but with no excess water showing on its surface.

If water runs out between your clenched fingers while you are squeezing, then the mix is too wet. Add more dry ingredients in proper proportion; if you have a little hypertufa left over you can always find another project to use it up. The proper degree of wetness, allowing for a little extra water to be further absorbed by the porous peat and perlite aggregates, should have just a little free water showing through the fingers of the fist clenched around the ball of hypertufa. Continue to test the mixture with the "squeeze method" after any further additions of wet or dry ingredients.

Once you obtain the correct balance of moisture, stop mixing. Overmixing incorporates more air into the mixture, which forms more pores in the hypertufa, lessening its strength.

Using a Cement Mixer

If you use a cement mixer to make hypertufa, the procedure is similar. After measuring the dry ingredients into the barrel, give the mixer several preliminary turns to mix them evenly. Then, with the barrel still rotating, begin to add the wet ingredients.

Here, it is definitely an advantage to use a hose, one with enough water pressure to project a strong stream of water into the barrel. Aim toward the top or back of the barrel, allowing gravity to help disperse the water evenly. As the drum rotates, the mixture inside will eventually form itself into many discrete, round "meatballs." At this "meatball" stage, the mixing process is just about complete. Check for moisture and workability in the manner mentioned above: you may need just a bit more water. Once the proper balance has been reached, *stop the motor*, carefully tip the barrel forward, and scrape the contents into a waiting container (the five-gallon bucket) positioned beneath the opening.

MAKING THE TROUGH

Once hypertufa has been mixed, it must be used immediately; so it is often advisable to make it in two batches. There is a learning curve with this, as with all crafts, and making the second batch will undoubtedly go more smoothly than the first. Making two batches instead of dividing a single batch prevents having half of a batch dry out while you are slowly and painstakingly packing the first half onto the floor of the trough.

Still wearing your sturdy rubber gloves (you can dispense with the dust mask and goggles once the dry ingredients have been moistened), begin to make the bottom of your trough.

Packing Hypertufa

At this point, the form or mold for your trough is ready: sitting on the plastic sheet, with both upon a board. The drainage hole forms are in place. Now take a handful of the hypertufa and pack it into a corner of the mold. Pack it in as tightly as you possibly can, using the heel of your palm or a balled fist; even so, you will probably still have to go back later and compress it some more.

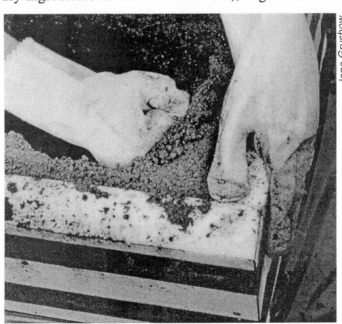
Jane Grushow

29

Get ready, then measure and mix the ingredients for hypertufa.

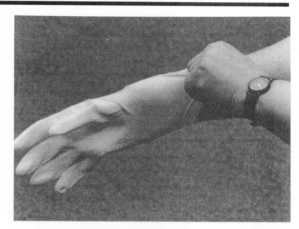

Photos by Jane Grushow

This is exactly how the hypertufa should look when it is ready to be packed into the mold: holding together in a clump, with no excess water showing.

Working the hypertufa, tamping it firmly to fill the mold.

The finished, textured hypertufa trough, well planted.

The object of all this packing and tamping is to make the hypertufa as solid, compact and air-free as possible, to make it more impervious to water. Tamping, besides removing air holes, causes the finest particles in the mix to rise to the surface. These can form a layer that will act like a fine glaze, to the point where a trough without drainage holes can become sufficiently watertight for a birdbath or small pool for bog and water plants.

Jane Grushow

Trough form with hypertufa floor and drainage hole form in place. Note the plastic mesh being cemented over the hole.

The strength of concrete depends not only upon the water/cement ratio, but also the degree of compaction. Holes, even minute bubbles, will later allow permeation of the trough by water which will freeze and thaw during the winter and cause eventual (though slow) disintegration of the trough walls.

Complete the four corners, then fill in the rest of the floor. Tightly pack the mix onto the floor of the trough, working around the drainage hole form. Work all the way around the floor and raise its height until it is all level with, or even slightly higher than, the hole. The drainage hole should be the lowest point of the floor. To aid in complete drainage, you can build the mix even higher in the corners, so that there is a slope running from the perimeter of the trough down to the drainage hole(s).

To test whether hypertufa has been sufficiently compacted, push your thumb into the floor: if it leaves a deep indentation, you have more pounding and compacting to do.

After completing the floor, begin building the walls. If you are using an interior form, place that form inside now. Begin filling the space between the interior and exterior forms with hypertufa mix, tamping it down tightly with a sturdy, mallet-like, flat-bottomed tamping tool (easily improvised). Work your way slowly around the perimeter, between the two forms, adding only an inch or two of height at a time. Be certain that the previous layer is as tightly tamped as possible, before placing the next addition.

Building walls by hand-packing, without an inner form, offers the best control. Begin by placing handfuls of mix on the floor against the inside of the wall form. Pack this in very tightly, to form a slightly flared buttress to support the rest of the wall. Work all the way around the perimeter, forming this base, before adding any height to the walls. Then begin adding hypertufa on top of this base, increasing the height of the walls in small increments, packing as tightly as possible against the walls. Press downward as well as outward. For maximum compaction, keep one hand on the outside of the wall, for support, as you press on the hypertufa from the inside (see photo, page 31). Work around the perimeter of the trough many times, building up the walls gradually, layer by layer, each layer secured and compacted before adding the next.

Try to keep the thickness of the walls consistent, and never make them any thinner than one inch. The one-inch thickness is appropriate only for troughs whose other dimensions are all less than 12 inches. Increase the thickness of the walls according to the overall volume of the trough.

The corners can be somewhat thicker, and rounded on the inside, in order to compensate for the amount that will be scraped away from the sharp, square outside corners during the finishing process. The walls should be thick enough to be stable and strong, but not so thick and chunky as to look clumsy. This, I'm afraid, is a subjective judgement.

If you need to stop during this process and leave the project for more than a few minutes, completely wrap your work-in-progress with the plastic sheeting, as well as covering any remaining hypertufa. When you return, the hypertufa may be retempered, if necessary, with additional water, to restore its plasticity and workability. Do not use hypertufa that is more than two hours old.

When you have finished building up the walls as high as you wish (and you need not always build to the top of the form), check over once again for complete compaction everywhere, using the thumbprint test. If you have been working with hypertufa for a while, or in the heat or sun or wind, and the surface has dried out somewhat, spray it over lightly with a mist of water, using either a plant mister or the hose on its finest, lightest setting. Then bring the plastic sheeting up and around the trough, enclosing it completely and taping it securely. If you have worked in a cool spot, in the shade, the trough can be left in place for its initial curing. If you have been working in the sun, move the trough, on its board, to the coolest, shadiest area.

The board is particularly handy at a group workshop, when the participants transport their troughs home to complete the curing and finishing.

Now go back and clean up your work area. Plastic sheets can be rinsed, dried and folded to be used again. All of the tools and containers (wheelbarrow, cement mixer, buckets) need to be washed out within an hour of using them, in order to keep the residues of hypertufa from hardening. Keep the containers in the shade, and covered with plastic, until you can get around to cleaning them. When the time comes to hose them down, carefully choose the site for dumping: do not flush out the containers onto a rhododendron bed, which would be hurt by the alkalinity of the mixture. However, the lawn just might benefit from the lime, sufficiently diluted.

Initial Curing

Careful *curing* will turn your damp hypertufa into an attractive and stonelike material. The process of curing is the replacement of the water-filled spaces in the mixture with the chemical results of the interaction of water and cement. Because curing occurs only in the presence of water (which is why it is also called hydration), it is most important to keep the trough well-sealed within its water-tight package of plastic.

The optimum conditions for curing are a temperature of 68 degrees F and a relative humidity of no less than 65 percent. Taking current and expected weather into consideration, position the trough. Remember, a great deal of damaging heat builds up within a wrapped container that is sitting in full sun.

The initial curing occurs in two stages. The initial "set" began almost immediately, certainly within the hour of your mixing the hypertufa—which is why it is so necessary to form the trough quickly. The final set can take up to seven days. During that time, the surface can be worked. This is the period during which you can change the texture, distressing and scarring it to make it resemble natural stone. The surface becomes less and less changeable during these seven days, as the setting continues.

Within 24 to 48 hours, the trough should be firm enough to hold its shape, if handled carefully. At this point, you can no longer make a dent in it with your finger, but you can scratch it with a tool. The amount of time needed to reach this stage varies, but a rule of thumb is that the larger the trough, the sooner it will be cured to this stage. Larger troughs, with greater mass, create more heat through the exothermic reaction of the cement and water which, in turn, speeds up the chemical reactions of the curing process.

FINISHING

In a large trough, the textural finishing can be done 24 hours after making the trough. For smaller troughs, allow at least an additional day, perhaps two. At this stage, after the initial curing period, the body of the trough holds together, and the surface will be workable enough to be textured with ordinary household tools. However, be forewarned that the cores of the trough walls have not yet completely hardened, and can still be broken by stretching (pulling at the sides) and jostling or jarring motions (you can guess how I learned this).

Jane Grushow

This hypertufa trough emerged from the mold with smooth sides and squared edges. Before it hardened completely, it was scraped, gouged, and textured to imitate horizontal stone strata.

The texture of this aged trough adds greatly to its charm.

Removing an exterior form made of foam insulation board couldn't be easier. Unwrap the plastic, but do not remove it, as you will need it again. Also, this would jostle the still-fragile trough. Remove the duct tape and discard. Pull out the nails and save them. Carefully peel away the foam board sides. Hose down the forms to clean them, and store them for re-use. For now, leave interior forms or any interior bracing in place, to add support for the trough walls during the subsequent "roughing up."

At this point, the sides of the trough will look slick and smooth, with some protruding tufts of fibers; all very hairy and unstonelike. Inspect all sides for any defects-cracks or gaps. You can repair them now (see page 45), either with hypertufa or cement, using a high proportion of liquid acrylic bonding agent: this is what it was made for. Or, if the cracks are not too large, or will not compromise the strength of the trough, you can leave them and play them up as part of the trough's character.

The first step in giving the trough a weathered and aged look is to remove the crisp, squared edges. Draw the edge of any sort of stiff blade or flat tool along the trough's edges to round them off. Begin with the top rim, inside and out: scrape and chisel until the edges have lost their sharp new look and appear rough and timeworn. Do the same to the four corners (this is why they were reinforced with additional hypertufa on the inside), top to bottom, and even along the edges of the trough's bottom.

Then the walls of the trough can be distressed and scored, using any number of different tools: a chisel, screwdriver, asparagus fork, old kitchen knife—anything that is stiff and sturdy, and not needed in the kitchen or workshop again.

The chisel can be used to imitate the vertical marks made when quarrying and carving real stone. Scouring that is more-or-less horizontal can imitate the striations of a sedimentary rock, like sandstone. And diagonal scoring could indicate that the trough came from a sedimentary formation that experienced geologic uplifting.

The walls of the trough can also be carved ornamentally: ancient Roman troughs have been found in England with a pattern carved on the sides. Troughs dating to the last century show simple frieze-like patterns covering portions of each of the four walls.

This process of "aging" will take a fair amount of your time and energy. It cannot be overdone: the more you work the trough, the older it will look. When you have finished carving and gouging and chiseling to your heart's content, brush the trough all over with a wire brush to further roughen up your own fresh cuts. Use a stiff brush or whisk broom to remove extraneous pieces that might still cling. As bits of excess hypertufa crumble off the trough and collect on the plastic sheet, be careful to save them. They make excellent mulch for your plants, one that will blend in well with the trough, giving a natural effect. Expect to see a fuzzy look from the exposed fibers; this will be handled later.

Final Curing

When the trough looks as old and as scarred as you want, and the excess bits have been cleared away, wet the trough once more, rewrap it in its plastic sheet, and store it safely, out of the sun, for 28 days—the long-term final curing.

This is the period during which the trough will reach its optimal strength. Tests have shown that concrete which is kept continuously moist for 28 days before it is again exposed to the air will have greater strength than will compounds cured for fewer days.

At the end of a month's time, unwrap the trough, removing any remaining braces and forms, and allow it to dry for a day or two. Once the trough has dried, burn off protruding fibers with a hand-held propane torch. Do not attempt this at an earlier stage in the curing, as any remaining moisture within the trough walls can expand explosively and cause cracks and gaps in the structure. For the same reason, keep the flame moving, not remaining at the same spot for more than a second or two.

At the end of all of this finishing, curing and drying, and depending on the time of year, the trough can be either planted up immediately or left to the elements for further weathering.

If you are planting lime-hating plants, it may be wise to apply a precautionary rinse of 90 percent water, 10 percent muriatic acid or vinegar to lessen the alkalinity of the new trough. Or let the rains weather the trough for a few more weeks or months. Trough pH, however, is less critical a factor than soil type.

If you are planning on leaving the trough outside over the winter, to weather further, be certain that the empty trough drains well: raise the trough off the ground with bricks or cement blocks to leave the drainage holes clear, and do not let fallen leaves or other debris prevent drainage.

That Fine Mossy Coating

Even after it has been planted, a new trough can look bare and raw. That much-coveted fine patina of mosses and lichens gives a trough its air of venerable antiquity. This can be acquired naturally, as airborne spores come to rest on the moist walls of the trough. To accelerate this process, mix up a slurry (pureed in a blender) composed of ground mosses in a base of some kind of acidic liquid, such as buttermilk or yoghurt. Paint this onto the exterior walls of the trough. Store it in a shady, moist spot, and moss will grow quickly. It is not necessary to resort to the sometimes-recommended feeding with natural organic fertilizers (such as cow dung) added to the slurry.

USING HYPERTUFA IN OTHER WAYS
Alternative Troughs

You have now completed the first step: you have made a basic, nicely proportioned trough, to plant according to your needs or whims.

The next step will be to expand your collection of these useful planters: you will find that one is never enough. Once you understand the basics of making a hypertufa trough, even a small basic trough can be modified in endless ways. Changes in size, shape, form, color and finish can be made at a number of points in the trough-building process.

Feet, like these by Roberta Berg, improve drainage while making a handsome trough accent.

Feet. Feet for the trough are not only handsome, but enhance drainage for the plants by lifting the base of the trough off the ground. If the feet are to be an integral part of the trough, this can be achieved in a few ways:

If the trough is being built upside-down, over an inverted form, build the feet on last, adding either square or round feet to the four corners of the top (which becomes the bottom of the trough).

However, when building the trough walls on the inside of a mold, you will need to take an additional piece of foam and make a false bottom for the trough. This piece is lain over the bottom layer of foam, and has holes in it where the feet will be. It should be of the same dimensions as the floor of the trough (the length and width of the inside of the form), and equal in thickness to the desired height of the feet.

For instance, if the feet are to support a 12- by 12-inch trough three inches off the ground, then the false bottom should be cut to 12 by 12 inches, and three or three and a half inches thick.

Parts of this false bottom are cut out in the desired shape and position for the feet: either four corners or two long sides; straight-sided or tapered. Pack the cutout portions with hypertufa first, very tightly. Then pack in hypertufa for the rest of the bottom of the trough, on top of the newly made feet and the false bottom.

A beaded edge. Another touch of refinement is a beaded edge (beading in the same sense as the woodworking term: a projecting rim, band or molding). Beading around the upper edge of a trough can either be built in, or built on. When working on the inside of a form, achieve the look of a beaded edge by adding a raised ridge (wood molding, wood putty or a hard plastic tubing) to the inside of the form, about an inch down from the top. This will then leave an indented impression all the way around the outside perimeter of the finished trough when the sides of the form are removed. Beading can be further refined and rounded during the finishing.

When building over the outside of a mold, the beading can be formed along the bottom (this becomes the top when the trough is finished) of the outside of the trough, as you begin to build the walls. This extra lip is made like a coil, applied to the bottom edge.

Ornamental objects—shells, stones, branches and leaves—can be attached to the insides of the trough form. These can either leave an indentation in the finished trough, or become a part of it, depending on how securely the object is attached to the form and whether the plan is to have the object leave an impression on the side of the trough or become embedded in it.

If there is to be an indentation carved or pressed into the side of the trough wall, be sure to compensate by building up the inside of the wall at that spot. Any thin spots in a wall will obviously be weak spots, compromising the strength and longevity of the entire trough.

Hypertufa Applied on Foam

For a rectangular trough that is even more lightweight and portable, the hypertufa mixture can be troweled on as a plaster-like covering for a Styrofoam™ box. Suitable foam ice chests are widely available. Those with smooth, straight sides are easiest to use. But note that it is harder to make a trough this way than to build one from scratch, unless you are used to the look and feel of hypertufa.

Prepare the surface by cleaning away any loose dirt or oily residues, which would keep hypertufa from adhering. When making a hypertufa mixture that is to be applied as a skin on an existing surface, be sure to use the liquid acrylic bonding agent. Use one part liquid acrylic to one part water, a 1:1 dilution. And because the skin or skim coat of hypertufa is not being used for structural strength, this mixture can be thinned more than usual with the water/liquid acrylic mix, making it easier to apply. It helps to make a hypertufa mix that is high in cement: one part cement to one part peat and another part perlite. Include fibers as well. Save a cup or two of the dry mixture in a tightly sealed plastic bag, in case you later need it for patching the finished trough.

Paint the sides of the foam box with a coating of undiluted liquid acrylic, then while it is still wet or tacky, apply the skim coat of hypertufa.

Extra texture can be incorporated as this is being applied: sand or fine gravel can either be incorporated or pressed into the finish while it is still wet. Texturing tools can create any desired patterns of ridges and irregularities.

Trowel and pat the hypertufa on, like plaster, around the exterior of the styrofoam box and up over the top edge. If the hypertufa does not stick well enough, add a little more cement. Continue this plastering for a few inches down into the interior of the box; the remainder will be hidden by soil and plantings.

A slow curing is even more necessary when the hypertufa is no more than a thin skin. Keep the entire trough wrapped and sheltered, to maintain a moist, warm (but not hot) environment. If the surface were to dry very quickly, it could shrink and pull away from the styrofoam base. Allow at least a week, longer if possible, undisturbed, for the hydration process to harden the cement-based mix.

Other Forms for Troughs

As mentioned, the polystyrene foam insulation board is an easy, but certainly not the only method of making a form for your trough. For a source of endless variations, you need only look around your home. Innumerable objects can serve as molds or forms for a hypertufa planter. They will be protected by the plastic wrapping. Baking pans (springforms with their release latches are ideal) or dish pans: oval, round, half-round (for a planter standing against a wall) or quarter-round (just what that bare corner needs).

Be sure to use sturdy pans, not disposable aluminum. Pans may be deep enough to hold a turkey, or as shallow as a pie plate. Shallow troughs are often used for exhibiting succulent plants, such as sedums and sempervivums. A birdbath is another natural use for this size and shape.

Consider using straight-sided souffle dishes, dog dishes, and stock pots; each provides essentially the same shape with differing proportions.

Other possibilities include:

- A ring mold, which will produce a planter to be used at the base of a picnic table's umbrella, or to hold a candle.
- Soup or salad bowls in family or individual serving sizes, or both.
- Small boudoir wastebaskets, which yield a deep planter ideal for weeping forms of dwarf conifers and willows, or tap-rooted woodies.
- A short, wide tumbler, which will yield a small tabletop planter, just the right size for forcing a few spring bulbs.

Special shapes can be rigged: if an oval platter has the shape you want, but not enough depth, turn it upside down over a pile of dampened sand that adds the necessary depth. The sides of this new form can be filled out with sand or a wide strip of metal flashing.

And, of course, your own existing pots and planters can be replicated in hypertufa: from deep long-tom pots to shallow bonsai containers. Clay, ceramic, or pressed peat containers abound at your local garden center. Garage sales and second-hand stores inspire ideas and supply found objects inexpensively. Any mold will yield two different-sized planters, depending on whether hypertufa is applied on the outside or the inside, so the possibilities stretch endlessly.

The whole process of working with hypertufa: building, initial curing, finishing, and final long-term curing, remains the same no matter the shape, and is covered by the previous instructions. But, if you plan to use any found objects, the tips on the next page should help.

Jane Grushow

Using Existing Objects as Molds or Forms

When using an existing container (anything from agate baking pans to pressed peat) as your form, you should provide a protective, impermeable layer between the form and the hypertufa. This shields the form from the alkaline mixture and prevents them from bonding together.

Wrap a sheet of plastic around the entire form, stretched as taut as possible and taped securely. The plastic should be thin enough to be flexible and closely follow the shape of the form, but not so thin that it will tear or leak. A large piece cut from a plastic trash bag is ideal, but not the filmy plastic covering from your dry-cleaned clothes. You will still need that additional sheet of strong plastic to enclose the trough and form for curing.

Wherever the plastic covering needs to be folded and pleated to conform to the shape of the mold, the folds should be securely taped down to keep hypertufa from slipping inside them. Any extra fold of hypertufa would pull away from the body of the planter as you unmolded it, leaving gaps and weak spots in the walls.

If you are working with a mold that is disposable, or will not be affected by the hypertufa, you can simply use a good coating of mineral oil, in place of the plastic covering, to help release the trough from its mold. This oil coating will work only if the mold is made of a non-porous material, such as metal, plastic, or glazed ceramic; use plastic sheeting over pressed peat and unglazed pottery containers.

Building a trough on the inside of any shape of form follows exactly the same procedure described for the basic square, made inside the foam insulation board mold.

It is often simpler to form a trough over the outside of an inverted mold, which also allows you to modify the texture of the outer walls as you build them. When using an inverted form, you will actually be working upside-down. You will be building the top edge of the trough first (which begins at the bottom of the form), and continuing upward, toward the bottom of the trough (which rests on the top of the form). If the inverted container is flexible, fill it with sand or something solid before you work, or it may squash out of shape.

You will need to form the top edge a bit thicker than you would normally want in the finished trough. This butressing gives the remainder of the walls a firm foundation, until the hypertufa has cured and hardened. Then, any excess thickness can easily be scraped away during finishing. Uneven edges are to be desired, not avoided, for a natural look.

Once this base (the top edge) of the planter is built and well compacted, the walls can be gradually added, up and over the form. Increase slowly, all the way around the form, about an inch or two of height at a time. Try to keep the thickness of the walls consistent. You can measure the thickness, as you work, by inserting a nail to guage the depth of various spots in the packed hypertufa (then be sure to patch them!).

When you reach the top of the form, place the hardware cloth (if you will be cementing it into place) on top of the form, and then the drainage hole form upon that. Continue to raise the level until hypertufa is packed tightly around the drainage hole. As a final step, assure the trough's stability by making the bottom flat and level. This can be done with a board and carpenter's bubble-level.

REPAIRING HYPERTUFA

Repairs can be made to hypertufa troughs fairly simply, at any point during their lifetime of use. Follow good practices for repairing any sort of concrete or plaster: begin by cleaning all loose material from the edges of the crack, scouring back to a firm, solid base. For minor cracks, use more of the hypertufa mixture, with an additional amount of liquid acrylic bonding agent to help strengthen the bonding of the new hypertufa with the old. Epoxies also work well.

In the case of larger cracks, or even splitting of the trough, a more aggressive approach is needed. Make the repair with mortar or a pure cement paste, again using the bonding agent to replace as much as half of the water. Paint the raw edges with undiluted liquid acrylic before applying the new mix. In all cases, the pieces of the trough should be bound tightly, with tape or straps, while this "glue" is curing or hardening.

MORE ON COLOR

After playing with and modifying the texture of the surface of a trough, there are many ways to change its look and coloring: either as part of the building process, or else during or even after the curing.

The internal colors, in both dry and liquid form, have already been discussed as an integral part of the hypertufa mix. These colors can also be used for pre-mixing with just the perlite, for those who simply can't abide the glaring white of the perlite, or to add a subtle color accent. Use integral colors to mimic the strata of natural rock and soil horizons by layering different tints of hypertufa as you build the trough. Insert single, thin lines of contrasting color, as Nature intrudes seams of molten materials between layers of rock. Mimic sharp white seams of calcite; dark seams of magma or layers of ash; streaks of colorful green serpentine; a rusty wash over rocks lying just below a rich seam of iron—all add to the attractiveness as well as the naturalness of this imitation stone.

After the curing stages, either initial or final, you can add color to the surface of the trough. Take advantage of the wide range of products used in the building industry to provide color to finished or partially finished concrete: shake-on colors; stains and washes; paints to be applied, then partially scrubbed or worn away. Any surface color that is applied after a trough wall has been stamped with patterns will pool in these concavities, heightening their decorative effect.

You can use one of the shake-on color products (or color/hardeners) while the hypertufa is still wet, if you have formed a trough using the upside-down method and the exterior walls are exposed. These come in an assortment of useful, natural colors. They can be used singly or in combination to reproduce the variety of colors inherent in natural rock.

These color/hardeners come as a powdered, cementitious material, which is shaken or troweled onto the wet surface of the hypertufa. The water already present in hypertufa activates the colors to form a strong bond with it. Because these colors remain on the surface, richer, deeper effects can be realized than with the integral tints. They also seal the surface, making the hypertufa more weather-resistant through freeze-thaw cycles, UV light, and exposure to de-icing salts. This surface can be further modified after curing, rubbing away the coating for a multi-layered, antique look.

Reactive surface stains are another alternative, used in place of or in combination with solid colors. These stains are acidic, water-based solutions of metallic salts, used after the final curing to produce a variegated, translucent layer of color. By using one or more stains (mixed together or applied in sequence), you can realize more subtly shaded variegated effects—very like natural stone. This is a good way to instantly achieve that desired time-wrought patina. Stains are applied either by painting and scrubbing into the dry hypertufa surface, or (for more even coverage) by spraying, using a hand-held plastic spray bottle. As they are acids, the stains will etch slightly into the surface, leaving behind pores, minuscule pockets in the finish, where the insoluble colors can pool. But this etching can also affect the ultimate weather-resistance of the planter. The building trade has overcome this problem, too, by developing finishing sealers, clear or colored, to match or contrast with the stain.

Any of these surface colorants can be used over a hypertufa project that has been previously tinted with an integral color. All of these products come with clear instructions for their use: adhere to them closely.

The mechanics of using special color finishes are simple, and the variety of effects infinite. Draw inspiration from rocks you see around your home (if you are so fortunate) and on your travels. Road cuts along the superhighways offer wonderful panoramas of geology.

Experiment with color combinations, and don't be afraid to go boldly: think of those stunning pink and black granites that occur from Maine's Cadillac Mountain to the Pamir ranges of Central Asia. Or the powerful intensity of the reds and rusts in the mountains of our Southwest.

OTHER USES FOR HYPERTUFA

After all the trough-building is done, any leftover hypertufa can be used to make auxiliary items for the trough or garden.

Rocks. Large or small fake rocks can be made by throwing handfuls of hypertufa onto a plastic-covered surface. Also, you can make a trough with built-in mounds of hypertufa, in order to create natural-looking mountain scenes with planting crevices as part of the container itself. This works especially well in a shallow trough, and can give stability to a very interesting vertical planting.

For deeper troughs, a "mountain" built up from the floor of the trough could displace too much of the planting medium and root run, and would require a good deal of hypertufa. In this case, it may be better to manufacture the rocks separately, and then place them in the soil just before planting.

Joyce Fingerut

These "custom rocks" can be made to suit each particular trough in terms of coloring, size, shape, and planting style. Planting holes poked into the rocks and crevices between rocks can be planned and created exactly where needed. Larger rocks can be built up by simply piling on additional rough handfuls of the mixture, until the desired size is reached (remembering that there will be some shrinkage with drying). Planting

Gravel-sized chips of hypertufa are great for mulching matching troughs.

pockets can also be made with a gouge or a chisel (very carefully) following the initial curing; or by drilling with a masonry bit at the end of the final curing.

Tabletop planter. A charming and naturalistic small planter, sized perfectly for a tabletop, can be made by beginning with a "thrown" free-style rock. Create a planting pocket by inserting a small plastic flowerpot (its exterior rubbed with mineral oil) into the wet hypertufa rock, sitting straight up or at a rakish angle. Create the drainage hole by using a pencil or stick to poke through the pot's own drainage hole and then out through the bottom of the hypertufa. The plastic pot can remain as part of the planter, be removed immediately after the impression has been made in the "rock," or (carefully) eased out after the first curing. This small planter will nicely showcase a group of the minor bulbs, making good use of the weather-resistant hypertufa.

Because these informally thrown rocks and planters are not as tightly packed as when tamping tightly into a mold, there are certain advantages and problems. The loose, informal structure looks more natural—very much like true tufa rocks. The many pores hold water, which will benefit the contained plants and also encourage the formation of that desired moss/lichen patina. However, this same porousness can also lead to the earlier disintegration of any planter left out to weather the winter. But, being so simple to make, they are easily replaced or repaired.

Security. For security from high winds in unsheltered positions (or fleet fingers in public places), a screw-eye bolt can be built into the sides or bottom of any trough while the hypertufa is still wet. After curing, the planter can then be secured, with wires, to something more permanent.

Garden ornaments. Not everything made of hypertufa has to contain plants. Use it as a form of weather-resistant clay, and mold decorative plaques or other whimsical creatures. Those small table-top planters can be built without a drainage hole and then filled with wax and a wick to create outdoor candles.

Joyce Fingerut

Decorative garden plaque created by Roberta Berg.

47

A carefully rounded and refined shape, with a slight indentation, can simulate the quiet shibui of a water-stone. In fact, hypertufa lends itself to replicating many lovely Japanese-style garden ornaments.

Joyce Fingerut

Japanese lantern made of hypertufa, by Roberta Berg.

Molds can also be combined for two- or three-part garden ornaments, such as a Japanese stone lantern. A tripod base is worked over an inverted pressed-peat liner for a hanging basket; the central core is a cylindrical shape, about the size of your average stock pot, with openings carved into two sides for the candle to shine through; all topped with a cap molded around a shallow pan or pie plate. Then, use that water-stone as the perfect accompaniment.

Supporting pillars for troughs can be made in the form of four feet, or two long bricks or flattened stones. When raising a trough, solid supports at the two ends will be sufficient for anything up to 15 inches in length; beyond that, a third support should be built and placed beneath the center of the trough.

Supports for troughs.

Fingerut

Pavers. Garden pavers and steppingstones can also be formed from hypertufa. They can be made in the standard way, on a worktable in a mold, or be created directly at the spot in the landscape where they are needed.

In this case, simply excavate the size(s) you need, to a depth of at least four inches. These holes need not be lined, but the earth beneath should be well compacted to support the walkway. Hypertufa is placed in the holes and tightly packed, as with any other project.

The exposed tops of the pavers need to be roughened and textured, with a stiff broom or a wire brush, to create a non-slip surface. This can also be accomplished by adding a rough aggregate, such as sharp coarse sand, fine grit or pebbles to the surface. Be sure to press the aggregate into the wet mixture, so that all the particles are surrounded by the paste. Each of the pavers should then be covered for about an hour, for a brief period of curing. As there can be no moving them to a sheltered position, you may need to shade the pavers from the bright sun so that they cure slowly and evenly. At the end of an hour, uncover the pavers and sweep with a wet brush or broom, until the aggregate is exposed but still firmly held in the hypertufa. Re-cover to retain the moisture for the remainder of the curing process, which, ideally, should last for two weeks.

Moving on

While we have been playing with hypertufa accessories, the troughs have been quietly curing. Assuming that it is now one month and a few days since they were made, let's admire them, and turn our attention to setting them into the landscape and filling them with appropriate planting medium and plants.

Chapter Three
Planting a Trough

Jane Grushow

Troughs can be used ornamentally or horticulturally. If you plan yours mainly for floral display, decide whether you want a knock-your-socks-off single burst of bloom, or a longer period of more modest bloom, ever-changing, with something blooming all the time, but not everything at once.

If collecting plants is your aim, or you are a specialist, your troughs will showcase the choicest, most miffy treasures—perhaps limited to one genus, or even a single species.

Whatever your goal, thoughtful preparation improves your results. A trough, or any container for plants, can provide the specialized conditions they need. But troughs and containers also raise problems by magnifying normal fluctuations of moisture and temperature. Shifts in temperature, which are absorbed and buffered by a large mass of open ground, have a more extreme effect on this miniature landscape. But note that the larger the trough, the less damaging the negative effect. Similarly, a small container gives up its moisture more easily, subjecting plants to stressful cycles of drought and moisture. These problems can be mitigated by careful design and planting, plus attentive, consistent care.

USING TROUGHS IN THE LANDSCAPE

Troughs are often made or acquired singly, and then sited in the garden, to stand alone. But they offer so much more when a few are grouped together and planted around, either as a feature complete in themselves, or integrated with existing features of the house or garden. You can plan, design, and construct a series of troughs in related and complementary sizes and shapes. Use these to frame an entryway, line a path, accent a formerly bland stairway, decorate that blank side-wall of the garage, or nestle into the top course of a dry stone wall.

The troughs that are home to miniature water gardens are right at home on the surround of a pool, especially one with stone coping or a slate deck. And, of course, troughs are the most natural way to augment your rock garden, expanding the garden onto a hardscaped area.

When using these groupings, as in planning any feature, it is wise to check all points from which they will be viewed, including the view from a sitting or standing position. In the latter case, they could be given extra height, to bring the plants closer to the viewer, by the use of pillars or a plinth of stone or (what else?!) hypertufa.

Will these troughs be seen while moving (as along a walk or flight of steps), when the viewer's attention needs to be grabbed on the fly and an impression made in the instant? Or will they rest on a patio where there will be plenty of time for contemplation of the subtleties of the plants and their setting?

The size and scale of the troughs and even the color of the plants can be selected, depending upon whether they will be viewed close up or from a distance, or even from inside the house.

A group of troughs need not contain all the same plants or planting design, unless repetition is used for emphasis, but there should be some underlying link among them. Whether this association is based on a visual scheme (repetition of flower color or leaf texture) or an intellectual theme (a collection of some taxonomic entity) is, naturally, the gardener's own decision.

Styles can either be strictly in keeping with surroundings, or deliberately contrasting. Lush, overflowing planters soften strong or ascetic modern lines while lean, spare, architectural plants make a bold statement in the midst of a cottagey landscape.

EXPOSURE

While there are any number of spots in the home landscape where a trough is desirable and attractive, there are a few locations that would be anathema to the health of the plants in that trough. Although some contained plants (such as woodlanders) might require shade, be aware that the shade under the overhang of a house is protected from rain as well as sun, and that a trough sited there will need to be watered by hand. This point reminds us to place the troughs where they can be easily reached by a hose.

On the other hand, bringing the trough out to just beyond the overhang will subject it to torrents of rain that pour off the roof, washing the plants right out of the trough. The same situations exist in the shade of trees with a dense canopy: dry at the interior and prone to washouts at the drip line.

Plants in a trough (especially high alpines) may require protection from winter rain. A slow but steady dripping on the tight bun of a dryland or montane plant will rot its center. This is especially true of those that cannot handle moisture during their dormant state. In this case, if the trough cannot be moved, some temporary structure must be set up on the trough itself (see page 64).

Returning to the issue of shade: what if none occurs naturally on your property? It is certainly easier, and far less expensive, to erect miniature shade-houses over individual troughs, or even several together, than to provide shade for an entire in-ground garden. You will want to be sure to tilt this cover (screening or lath) to correspond to the angle of the sun at the hottest hours of the day, during the warmest months of the year—at your specific latitude. There are books available with this information neatly calculated for you.

Or you can plant the shade right within the trough, allowing some taller sun-lovers to cast shade over more delicate, low-growing plants behind them.

And then there is the question of light. How much? What kind? And how is the amount of light related to the amount of heat it will generate? Of direct sunlight, the kindest is eastern, morning sun. In the afternoon, it can become harsh and drying during the summer months. Even succulent and dryland plants appreciate some protection from the sun during the hottest part of the day, especially at their roots.

Indirect light is another factor in the total environment of the trough and its plants. A trough placed in front of a south-facing wall that is light in color, such as light stucco or white siding, will receive reflected light on the rear of the plantings, as well as sun from the south. This all-around light can be very good, or it can be a problem, but it should be taken into account.

A dark surface, too, is significant. A trough situated next to a blacktop driveway will have to contend with ambient heat radiating from that dark mass.

Water presents its own set of factors to deal with: is the site well drained, or will the trough need to be raised on pillars so that water does not back up into it? The need for a hose has been mentioned, but take extra care in watering the trough, so that a harsh jet of water does not wash the plants, soil and mulch out of the container. Deflect the stream by aiming it at one of the rocks; better yet, use a softer setting and water with an oscillating motion.

After doing your reading, do not unquestioningly accept the dictum that such-and-such a plant simply needs sun or shade, because there are infinite degrees of each. Sun in northwest North America (even at its most intense) can hardly be compared in effect to the light found in the Southeast, or on a high plains plateau. In any setting, morning light is kinder than intense afternoon sun; and plants everywhere could probably benefit from some protection against the summer's afternoon glare.

Shade is equally variable. Compare the difference between the year-round solid shade on the north side of a building with the dancing, lacy shadow of a locust tree. You need to understand your plants and know your climate. Then you can custom design your own environmental niche.

Rex Murfitt

This saxifrage thrives in a sunny exposure with rocky protection for roots.

Although it would be easiest to say that you should not use a trough in problem areas, these are precisely the spots that need a container, since they will not easily support in-ground plantings. So take all factors into account and compensate for them. Container planting is ideal for catering to plants' special needs.

COMPANION PLANTINGS

Once you have satisfied the requirements of the plants within the trough, the next concern is to tie it visually to its surroundings. Whether sited in the garden or against a paved backdrop, there could be companion plants growing around the perimeter of the trough.

These companion plants "front down" the trough; that is, act as a visual link, an intermediate size of plant, between the trough's edge and the ground, especially for those troughs raised on blocks to prevent backsplash. These plantings can either repeat or complement those within the trough. Another *Dianthus simulans*, for example, that is planted directly beneath one that is growing over the edge of the trough will create the impression that the plant has been happy enough in its trough home to seed itself around. A colony of plants always provides an air of horticultural exuberance.

Joyce Fingerut

A dwarf conifer will balance and extend the solidity and visual weight of the trough itself. And here is an opportunity to grow some of the relatives of the plants represented in the trough: those slightly more aggressive species or larger cultivars. And moss (or a mossy *Sagina*) always helps to knit planter and surroundings into one.

Where a trough is used on a cement-based area, or in a corner where there is no other opportunity for planting, devise some way of providing a context for it. This can be done by using additional, smaller containers having a similar type of planting; or perhaps a related accessory, such as a shapely stone, or a base of gravel mulch or a stone plinth.

Any slate or brick patio, laid dry, offers the ideal opportunity for such companion plantings. Lift some of the slates or bricks, and rest the trough on the bare soil; perhaps improve this soil to provide a more agreeable home for the plants. Nestle a fastigiate, but dwarf, conifer against one corner of the trough and underplant that with one or two buns. Add mat-formers around the other sides of the trough and you have a rich, complex, and interesting scene.

Some of the finest public examples of this type of planting can be found in the Royal Botanic Gardens at Edinburgh in Scotland and at Wisley, in England.

SOIL: PROVIDING THE IDEAL PLANTING MEDIUM

The two most basic needs of plants are for moisture and air. So it stands to reason that the soil (technically known as the "root substrate," since the best planting medium may contain no actual soil) must be composed of two basic components: one that retains moisture and one that allows the excess moisture to drain away, leaving behind open pores of air. These usually are materials that are vegetable (moisture-retentive) and mineral (non-absorptive, to enhance drainage). The organic base can be provided by any of a number of materials: leaf mold, or composted materials such as peat, coir and well-aged manures. Use whatever is at hand and free of pathogens and weed seeds.

Drainage materials can be any hard, impervious minerals, crushed but not too fine. This free-draining mineral component can be composed of sands (such as those used for sand-blasting or swimming pool filters) or grits (for the crops of turkeys and chickens), or crushed stones of varying diameters.

Materials that fall between the two types are perlite, vermiculite, and calcined clay particles (clay that has been baked and then ground), all of which hold small amounts of moisture within their porous structures, but function essentially to enhance drainage.

The term "perfect drainage" is thrown about, sometimes along with phrases such as "perched watertable," "porosity," "crocks," and "columns," often accompanied by little or no explanation. In his writings on the subject, Jim Borland, of Denver, Colorado, emphasizes the necessity of good drainage for good root aeration. He discusses the way soils act in the open garden and in a container, and why the best soil for one is unsuitable for the other.

Plants restricted to a planter must deal with the conditions they're given. The stresses of life in a container are many and varied: wide swings in temperature, quick evaporation of moisture, and poor siting. Garden soil used in a planter often brings soil-borne pests and diseases.

The structure of the soil in which the plants must live is equally important. Containers require an "open soil" that contains enough pore spaces between the molecules of soil for the plant roots to take in fresh air and expel waste gases. The necessity for air is as critical as that for water and nutrients. The best soil structure for healthy plants is one that contains the ideal balance of moisture-

creating and planting garden troughs

Rocks, planting medium, mulch and moss, ready for a trough.

Jane Grushow

retentive particles and air-filled pores. This is not achieved by combining many additives of various sizes. As you recall, the recipe for concrete called for well-graded aggregates because having a wide range of particle sizes means that there will be a particle of aggregate to fill every size of pore, thus ensuring the most tightly compacted material with the fewest pores. This is, most emphatically, what you do not want for your plants.

Keep your ingredients down to two or three: you can pair peat with perlite or coir with sand for a favorable combination. A mixture of humus, sand, and grit is the most popular combination for a lean rock garden planting medium. There are almost as many planting recipes as there are gardeners. And the types and proportions of the ingredients are very plant- and site-specific. For instance, the sort of mixture that will keep alpine plants happy is commonly agreed to be one that is well-drained. However, the degree of drainage needed will differ greatly, depending on whether the gardener is growing these plants in Seattle (with about 34 inches of rain a year, falling mostly in the winter, when alpines are least tolerant of wet conditions) or in Minneapolis (which receives five inches less, mostly in the summer, but with winter precipitation generally in the form of protective snow).

A soil appropriate for bog or woodland plants will be heavy with humus and other organic materials, while the leaner alpine mixes will be composed of a greater proportion of drainage materials. Regionally, plants growing in containers in the relatively cool, moist Northwest will demand a quick-draining mixture, as compared with the moisture-retentive mix needed in the hotter, drier or windier climates of the South and Midwest.

Plant choice affects the choice of soil. Calcicole plants prefer a high percentage of lime, and calcifuge plants are lime-haters which need an acid soil. The pH, like drainage, is mostly based upon the mineral portion of the mix: calcareous limestones and tufa, or acidic granites and sands. Peat is generally regarded as the most convenient organic supplement for acid-loving plants.

Nutrients should be applied according to the nature of the plants and local weather patterns. Many commercial soilless mixtures already contain some basic trace minerals, but further nutrients will eventually be needed.

Annuals need a strong and continuous infusion of fertilizer to maintain their show of blooms throughout the growing season. This is even more important in a wet climate where nutrients are perpetually leached out with the rains. At the other extreme, an alpine plant, growing in a dry climate, needs very little to sustain itself. In fact, too high a fertility will result in growth that is leafy, lush, and out of character. Without the buffering rains to dilute and spread them through the soil, fertilizers' salts can burn vulnerable root hairs.

DEPTH OF SOIL

Providing proper drainage and moisture for plants in troughs can present a problem. In his lectures and articles about the water and air capacities of containerized soils, Jim Borland has stressed that the drainage characteristics of a soil are directly and positively related to the depth of that soil. This "column" of soil is radically shortened when moving from the theoretically limitless depth of the garden to the measurable shallowness of a container. Gardeners unwittingly cause further problems for their plants by using a layer of "crocks" in the bottom of the containers, based on the widespread but mistaken belief that this extra layer of porous materials will enhance the soil's drainage. In fact, the opposite is true: that by placing a layer of "drainage material" beneath the soil in a container, the gardener is shortening the depth of the soil, and as a result, impeding drainage rather than enhancing it.

That area where the soil ends, whether just above the bottom of the pot or above the layer of drainage material, contains the wettest soils. This is because the water is pulled downward by gravity, to accumulate at the lowest point. The crocks create a barrier to the water's passage, at least until a critical mass of water builds up from above. This area of high moisture content is referred to as the "perched water table." By creating a shallower column of soil, the gardener is artificially raising the level of that saturated soil closer to the roots of the plants.

The container's full depth is needed, therefore, in order to keep this area of saturated soil away from the plants' roots and crowns. This will provide the plants with improved drainage, as well as a greater supply of nutrients and an improved root run. Once the accumulated water reaches the bottom of the container, good-sized drainage holes in the floor of the trough permit the excess to exit freely. The screens placed over those drainage holes will keep the planting medium from flowing out with it.

ROCKS

In addition to plants and soil, the most common element in a trough is rock. Rocks of all sizes and types: from solid granite hulks to smaller chunks of precious tufa, with their porousness that is so congenial to plant roots.

The most appropriate rock to use is either found in your own locale or in the plants' native habitat. They are more than decorative. Rocks in a trough fulfill the same role as in nature: they create small-scale ecosystems. It should be noted that, by displacement, they decrease the amount of space available for

Rex Murfitt

Draba rigida, enhanced by the rocky structure within the trough.

plants. However, their presence improves growing conditions by slightly moderating extremes of temperatures with their mass, and providing the cooler root run that most plants enjoy. Rocks channel valuable rainwater down their sides directly to plant roots, and can help deflect water from the hose so that it does not rearrange plants, mulch, and soil.

And then there are micro-niches created around the perimeter of any rock: full and reflected sun to its south, which is moderated to a half day on either side, with shade in its lee. Rocks of many forms are stable, year-round features, practical and artistic anchors for alpine plants. Use a large monolith: craggy, scored and scoured. Or set in a combination of smaller stones, placed to mimic a series of uplifted ledges, or scattered and buried as if outcrops in an alpine lawn.

As you plan, remember that you are trying to replicate a few square inches of alpine landscape, not the whole mountainside.

Rex Murfitt

In lieu of rocks, especially in the recreation of a woodland, pieces of wood, carved by decay, enhance the composition and at the same time supply nutrients continuously as they decompose. Where rocks are not available or desired, similar visual weight can be provided by a nicely congested dwarf conifer.

Rocks and plants must be culturally compatible. Do not use limestone rock with ericaceous plants, which require an acid soil to extract the nutrients they need. However, the case against the reverse (lime-lovers with acidic granite) is not as compelling, as these plants are generally more adaptive.

Now, having reviewed choices of planting medium, and drawing from the options listed in the plant listings in the next two chapters (or sitting in your own holding frame, awaiting planting), let's bring it all together: plants, materials, and trough-planting technique.

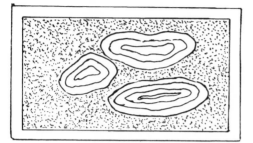

Three large rocks
positioned to form
tight planting
crevices.

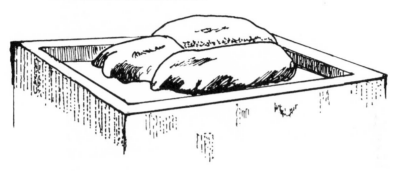

Several smaller stones
grouped to form an open
planting area.

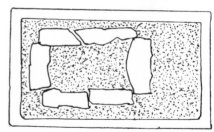

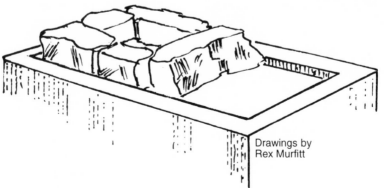

Drawings by
Rex Murfitt

stabilize it while you are adding the next plants. Continue planting and back-filling. Plants at the edge of the container can be inserted at a reclining angle to encourage them to weep over the sides and soften the edges of the planter.

Then fill the trough with medium up to about an inch below the rim, to allow enough room for mulching the plants.

Now water in the entire planting, waving a light spray of water back and forth over the trough, to avoid washing out any of the soil or plants. This should settle things in nicely. If needed, add more soil so that the level remains just below the crowns of the plants. These crowns should rise cleanly above the soil, and will eventually be protected by mulch.

The horticultural value of mulch around the plants is not in dispute; however care should be taken to coordinate the type of mulch with the plants and their setting. The appropriate material to mulch a collection of shade plants would be organic, such as finely ground bark chips or well-shredded leaves. Keeping in mind the relatively small scale of the trough and its plants, you should use mulch of a fine texture.

In an open, sunny location, using alpine or dryland plants, the mulch should be composed of fast-draining mineral grit. Small (3/8") river-stone jacks and rough grits are appropriate for montane settings. Use a coarse sandy or limy material for dry lowlanders and Mediterranean plantings. Those bits of hypertufa that were left over from the process of roughing and finishing the trough will work beautifully here, being

Rex Murfitt

Anacyclus depressus mulched with grit.

culturally and aesthetically tied to the trough and its contained plants. Using two different sizes of stones or grits will give everything a more natural look. Apply mulch about an inch deep. Cover the entire surface of the soil, around the plants' crowns and among the rocks. Renew it each year, if necessary.

At this point, water everything in again, lightly. It is vital that the recently disturbed roots be settled into the new soil as soon as possible, particularly if the weather is sunny. This initial watering is critical; water must penetrate through the soil to the bottom of the trough, moistening all the soil as it passes through. When water can be seen trickling from the drainage hole, it is safe to assume the soil is moistened throughout. Nevertheless, it is advisable to dig little holes here and there on the surface, to check that water has spread evenly throughout the trough; there should be no dry corners.

Water must be given plenty of time to work its way into the soil. Therefore, use a watering can with a fine rose and gently water: this is the only sure way to soak the soil and not spoil your work by washing the soil from the landscape. Apply just enough water until you see runoff starting, then stop until it soaks in.

From then on occasional trimming or training may be in order. Trees and shrubs can be clipped or trimmed. The word pruning is avoided, as it gives the wrong impression; all that is required is minimal shaping and direction control. For example, where a plant is expected to grow to the edge and then drape over the side, it is often necessary to trim the inner growth to encourage it in the direction you wish. Pine trees can be guided by judiciously pinching back the candles (new green growth). Many species look untidy after flowering; by removing spent flowers and stems, the symmetry of the "bun" is regained.

The question of fertilizer is of concern; usually it can be relegated to the back burner for about two years. The original soil mixture has sufficient nutrients to maintain the limited diet best for the slow development of alpine plants. Eventually, the soil will become depleted by the demands of the plants and by leaching from watering and rainfall. When this stage is reached, growth will stop and the time to consider fertilization has arrived. Select one that is low in nitrogen, as lush green growth is not acceptable. Organic fertilizers, such as bone meal, with its low analysis and slow breakdown, are ideal. Some gardeners use the slow-release products such as Osmocote™ 10-10-10.

Wait until the flower display is over before applying fertilizer: remove most of the gravel mulch and apply a modest dressing of fertilizer, working it into the surface soil. This is the time to add more soil to any low areas that may have developed. Replenish and replace the topdressing and the mulch. Follow up with a good watering.

This snow-covered roof helps to protect the trough from wetness in winter.

Winters are the trough gardener's greatest trial; the hot sun of summer can be moderated by taking advantage of shade. Excessive winter rains can be mitigated by devising various shelters of glass or plastic. A heavy winter-long snowfall can be a blessing, as the insulating blanket protects the troughs and living contents from the bitter cold. But, short of moving troughs into the protection of sheds, garages, frames and greenhouses, there is little that can be done to lessen the effect of extreme winter weather. Putting up screens to deflect the wind is a help, for it helps ward off dessication. Bales of hay or straw packed around troughs as mild insulation serve the same purpose. The simple practice of laying a covering of conifer branches on the troughs is very effective against wind and sun. All efforts will fail if the plants are not hardy enough for the climate. Gardeners have a tendency to "push the envelope" when it comes to hardiness.

Here are a few thoughts on overwintering that may be of value.

- Use species that are hardy in your area.
- Do not try to prevent freezing.
- Once frozen, it is better that plants remain so for as long as possible.
- Keep frozen troughs in the shade, if possible: it lessens temperature fluctuations.
- Where practical, overwinter troughs in the protection of a shelter.
- Check protected troughs for drought: during periods of freezing and thawing the soil will become dry.
- Water only during "open" spells, when soil is not frozen.

Now you are probably ready, or even itching, to decide about what to plant in your troughs. The next two chapters provide solid guidance for plant selection, with general guidelines as well as examples and names of plants to seek.

Betty Mackey

Chapter Four
Plants for Garden Troughs

Rex Murfitt

There is no such thing as a "trough plant."

However, it is true that there are lots of plants that will live and grow happily in a trough and other plants that may be persuaded to live in a trough by a gardener's skill. Favorite examples from among the many appropriate choices are described in the discussion of plants starting on page 73.

Traditionally, old sinks and animal feeding troughs are planted with alpine plants, as these are small plants, capable of living contentedly in a limited space, all the while providing a display of brightly colored flowers. Alpine gardeners often plant their rare or choice plants in troughs where they can provide special soil mixtures and meet other requirements of these treasured plants, and showcase them at the same time. The trough garden also provides a safe haven for small plants that may easily be lost or overwhelmed in the open garden.

Alpine landscapes are not the only option. Almost any garden design can be tried, if its elements are in scale with the trough. Dwarf roses have been used, laid out in miniature formal rose beds. The English gardener, Anne Ashberry, wrote a little book entitled *Miniature Gardens*, published in 1954, in which she describes several of her own little gardens. They sound like fun, with miniature trellis work and crazy paving, and even small pools and streams. Her lawns are portrayed by tiny, low-growing, grasslike plants.

Ordinary garden plants are sometimes used in troughs, though rock gardeners may consider them inappropriate. I once saw a display of pink petunias flourishing in an antique hand-carved trough, so perfectly placed that the bright flowers glowed amid the gray stone walls of the cottage garden.

67

Troughs are most frequently planted with hardy perennials, either those retaining their growth all year round, or those whose living stems die down each winter to a hardy rootstock, which then produces new stems and leaves the following spring. Small trees and shrubs, bulbs, and certain annuals may also be appropriate in some situations.

In all cases, the essential consideration is that plants be naturally dwarf and slow-growing, with small leaves and branches. Even the flowers will be in keeping if they, too, are small. Ideally, trough gardens are planned to be long-term projects and, once planted, should remain undisturbed for several years. Plants that threaten to outgrow their allotted spaces will have to be removed, as they will soon engulf their smaller neighbors.

The limited amount of soil that a trough contains is also a factor; plants have to be able to prosper within this restriction. Moreover, trough gardens are expected to stay outside all year round; therefore, the plants must be able to withstand winter cold. In addition to cold, they are often required to endure high summer temperatures. Heavy fall and winter rain can result in root rot or foliage decay, caused by long periods of water-soaked soil. In hot climates such as those found in the southern United States, very few alpine plants can survive, yet sedums and succulents, cacti, and various species of dwarf plants can be grown in free-draining soil for successful troughs.

Whatever our climate and growing conditions, we make great demands of these little plants for our troughs. From early spring, through the summer and even into the fall, we expect masses of bright, colorful flowers; the winter months too, if we can manage it. Moreover, these plants must be of neat and tidy habit, and maintain foliage that is pleasing to the eye all year round. Finally, we expect them to be durable, perennial and to live forever. This is a lot to expect from a group of plants when so little is offered in return. Therefore, we must undertake much of the responsibility for their success and health, by selecting carefully those plants we expect to work so hard for us.

LOCATING PLANTS

The mountain ranges of the world have been the original source of plants, and inspiration, for troughs. There we find many plants that are naturally dwarfed and thrive under spartan conditions. Above all, alpine plants are noted for their brilliant flowers.

It is no longer ecologically desirable, necessary or efficient for gardeners to go into the mountains and seek them out, for these plants have been grown and loved for many years and have become well established in the nursery trade in North America and Europe. This long alliance gardeners have had with alpine plants has contributed to the quality and variety that have been and continue to be introduced into cultivation. Selection and breeding have made available larger flowers and even double-flowered forms; and have opened ranges of color to the gardener, where previously the choice was limited to one.

Local garden centers and nurseries offer a wide selection of plants today, far more than a few years ago. Uncommon and very choice plants can be found regularly on the sales benches. Be a regular visitor during the season and check on any interesting new shipments that arrive. Soon you will be recognized by

PLANT TALK:
RECOMMENDED
PLANTS FOR TROUGHS

Rex Murfitt

THE CUSHION PLANTS

The cushion plants are the first plants visitors notice in a trough garden, or any collection of alpine plants. These neat domes of hard, tight foliage are irresistible. They are commonly called cushion plants because that is what they look like: some will grow as big as a real armchair cushion, while others remain the size of the top of a boiled egg. More often than not, they remind people of old-fashioned buns, and the best plants for the trough should be about the same size as the good old currant bun! The nursery in England where I was a student had an alpine house devoted to plants of this type; not surprisingly, it was known as "The Bunnery."

These plants embody all the appeal of alpine plants: small compact plants with lots of bright flowers and tiny leaves held closely to the plant, with almost no stems or twigs. Foliage is often silvery or white, due to masses of hairs which clothe the leaves. These hairs protect the plant from the harsh conditions of the mountains, where hot sun and drying winds will rob the plant of its essential moisture. The same hairs also will function to repel excessive water, which can threaten to suffocate leaves or penetrate and rot the plant's center—these are dryland plants. Moreover, this mat of hairs will trap a layer of air for the plant, when the foliage seems otherwise soaked.

Many cushion plants live in and on the boulder fields, crags, ridgetops, screes and similar places where some of the world's worst weather exists. These are tough places to be in stormy weather; even the winter snow is blown clear, robbing plants of their insulating blanket. I have seen cushion plants in full flower in crevices on the way up to the Jungfrau: it was raining and sleeting, and so cold and wet that my fingers could hardly operate the camera. But the moisture just beaded up on the dome of foliage and rolled off.

The mountain ranges of North America also have their share of wonderful cushion plants; some are easy to cultivate and others are not. The Great Basin, the grasslands of the Great Plains, the high deserts and steppes of the West, the great chain of the Rockies and many other places all have populations of buns and cushion-forming plants. Not all by any means are tiny domes. Some will grow from cushions into carpets turning into a mass of flower. The art of cultivating these so-called dryland plants is an absorbing pastime, capable of leading the gardener into a totally fascinating area of gardening, whether in a trough or not.

Androsace

Rock jasmines, as the androsaces are sometimes called, are members of the great primrose family, the *Primulaceae*. This important plant family also provides the many exquisite primulas, as well as other lovely alpine plants: *Cyclamen, Soldanella, Douglasia* and America's own *Dodecatheon,* known as the shooting star. Androsaces are widely distributed throughout Europe, Asia and North America.

Not all androsaces grow in the high fastness, but the smallest forms are limited to the mountain heights. As they descend in altitude, the species change, becoming somewhat taller, less dome-like, and more tufted, while some species throw out stolons and make a mat of silvery rosettes with an abundance of lovely pink heads of flowers. Species from the lower elevations are somewhat easier to cultivate in the trough garden than those from the highest altitudes, and provide some very pretty plants.

It is always a dilemma whether to mention these plants, since they are not always easy to buy and can be very hard to grow. On the other hand, if they are not discussed, how will gardeners ever get a chance to at least try them, even if they do not survive for long. Who is to say that there might not be a gardener with just that special touch needed to succeed? Secondly, why deprive gardeners of an opportunity to enjoy the fun and the challenge.

Rex Murfitt

Androsace sempervivoides

Too few nurseries are able to supply them, and those that can may find that androsaces are like some wines and do not travel well. Even a plant received in good condition may grow for a season then suddenly die. But, at least it is better to have tried and failed, than not to have tried at all. There is a good deal of pleasure in searching for sources of material and the anticipation of the arrival of plants and seedlists. Then there is the day the plants or seeds actually arrive. There is nothing to beat the satisfaction of seeing the first batch of tiny seedlings coming up in a pot, especially after the long wait. Sometimes the seeds will not germinate until the second year after sowing, so never throw away a pot of seed that has yet to germinate.

In their natural habitat, androsaces are much like some of the cushion saxifrages, preferring the crevices. Where they may be found growing in less precipitous places, in what might be called "soil," this is often nothing more than shale and gravel.

To expect any success growing androsaces, the trough must be in an ideal position with just the right amount of sun and shade. It will need enough sun to keep the plant short and compact, not too much or it will scorch. But too much shade will etiolate the plant, a condition that spoils the compact character and weakens tissues so they are susceptible to any passing disease.

Now that I have warned of all the drawbacks, let us look at a couple of *Androsace* species that might be a little more accommodating. *Androsace pyrenaica* is probably the best one to start with. It is a small plant with tiny green foliage, covered with fine gray hairs. The individual rosettes are crowded into a tight rounded bun. If and when it becomes established, spring will see it cover itself with a mass of yellow-eyed, white flowers on the tiniest of stems.

There are a few hybrids between *A. pyrenaica* and another widely distributed European species, *A. carnea*. These hybrids often will have pink, yellow-eyed flowers in addition to the white. Some have been named and appear periodically in nursery lists. On American lists, you are likely to find *A. x 'Millstream'*, or it may be listed as Millstream Hybrid; as long as the name Millstream is used, it will likely be the true plant. The name is taken from a garden in Connecticut, where it was discovered as a chance seedling in the alpine house of Mr. and Mrs. H. Lincoln Foster. These plants show the *A. pyrenaica* heritage in the foliage by their green leaves, with a touch of gray from the shortened hairs on the leaf surfaces. The plant will form a mound, although the habit is slightly less compact or crowded; nonetheless, these hybrids warrant a place in any trough garden.

The other parent, *A. carnea,* is itself very variable and several geographic forms are sufficiently different to warrant their being given the rank of subspecies. They are considerably easier to grow than the real buns and are more like tufted little plants than pure buns. They are composed of rosettes of short, spiky, awl-like leaves, which are green, with or without hairs. The silky character of massed hairs is absent. Flower stems vary from two to three inches and bear several flowers in an umbel (an umbrella-shaped cluster of florets whose spreading stalks arise from the apex of the stem). *A. carnea*'s short, tufted foliage will make a mossy cushion with flower stems up to two inches topped by umbels of soft pink flowers. *A. c. 'Laggeri'* is a particularly lovely shade of deep pink. When raised from seed, this species will produce seedlings that will vary in height and color; there will be a number of white-flowered forms, also. When growing for the trough garden, it will be necessary to discard those plants that look as if they may be too robust: sometimes seedlings will produce flower stems that are taller than normal. There is nothing wrong with them, but they might unbalance the scale of the smaller-flowered plants in the trough.

Draba

Many of the drabas make excellent subjects for the miniature garden because they, too, have a neat and appealing appearance. They are fun plants and very satisfying, as they are not as demanding as the *Androsace*. The color of the foliage that comprises the buns may be bright apple-green or a dark and lustrous green. Several lovely species have silvery, gray-green leaves, owing to the presence of silky hairs upon the leaves. Most flowers are yellow and will include a spectrum of shades and hues, so monotony of color is not a problem. Some varieties have heads of flowers dancing on threadlike stems, while others have no stems at all, with the flowers perched upon the surface of the bun. One or two species have white flowers.

Rex Murfitt

A dome-shaped draba in bloom.

Drabas bloom very early in spring and are a welcome sight with their dainty flowers brightening the garden. Coupled with domes of iron-hard rosettes, they suggest the austere conditions of the high alpine tundra. Drabas are spread across the mountain ranges of the Northern Temperate Zones; a few species occur in South America. The choicest species originate in the higher mountain ranges. It is difficult to believe that these tiny little alpine flowers belong to the same botanical family as the cabbage (the crucifers). For proof, examine a single blossom of each plant and note that in both cases the four petals are arranged in the shape of a cross.

In the wild they can be found growing in crevices and among broken rocks, or in open alpine meadows and scree slopes, within communities of other dwarf plants. In the Bighorn Mountains of Wyoming, they can be found growing among such lovely plants as the marvelous blue of the alpine forget-me-nots, *Eritrichium* spp., and the powder blue of the tiny columbine, *Aquilegia jonesii*. Here, too, dwells *Androsace chamaejasme* with its white flowers on silvery mounds.

In this environment, life is hard and summer short. During spring and early summer, soil moisture is plentiful and drainage is rapid: these are the conditions we should try to copy in the garden. These tough little plants will tolerate hardships, but will not withstand endless days of heat and high humidity, nor will they tolerate total drought.

It would be simple to say "go ahead and plant any draba you can find" in the sink or trough garden; unfortunately, this is not possible as there are around 300 species known and listed. Many of these are worthless as garden plants: some are annuals and of little floral value, and some even tall weeds. Even with a wide choice, the trough gardener will encounter the problem of ultimate size. Many species, while excellent in the rock garden, will be too large for a trough. Moreover, there is always the gamble that the plant you have obtained

G. acaulis is the species people usually picture in their mind's eye whenever gentians are mentioned. This is the species regularly seen on Swiss calendars and chocolate bars, with its huge upturned trumpets of superb blue. In the interests of accuracy I will explain that the name acaulis means stemless; yet the gentians usually grown in gardens have short stems. Some of mine have leafy stems up to two inches long. It is generally agreed today that the name *G. acaulis* is a group name that encompasses several European species that have similar botanical attributes.

Should you see offered in a list the names *Gg. alpina, angustifolia, clusii* or *dinarica*, do not miss the opportunity to acquire them. You will not be disappointed. They are all magnificent, each with its distinctive differences.

Those who live where there is a cool fall, have a trough that they are prepared to dedicate to one species, and are prepared to buy from western mail-order nurseries can have a spectacular display of pure gentian blue right up until the first killing frost or the heavy duty fall rains set in. This is achieved by acquiring *G. sino-ornata*, the fall-blooming Chinese gentian.

Before reaching for the catalogs, be sure that your native soil contains no lime and your water supply is also lime free. Then prepare a richer soil mixture than normal trough soils, with a basis of good loam, some organic matter, and some very coarse sand with lots of small gravel in it. It is worthwhile to screen this gravel through a fine sieve to remove excess dust and silt, often referred to as fines. Planting is best accomplished early in spring, just as the green shoots begin to appear.

Good sized plants may be spaced as far as six inches apart. During the summer, soft, grassy-looking, floppy stems sprawl over the surface, often growing together in a tangle. Keep them from exposure to drying winds and sun; partial shade will be sufficient. They will demand that the soil be moderately moist: never let it become totally dried out for any length of time. Then in late summer or early fall, terminal buds, one to a shoot, begin to appear until the foliage disappears beneath a haze of azure-blue trumpets. There are several hybrids within the Asian gentian species, and they are not at all easy to find. Therefore, accept any fall-blooming gentian you are offered.

Penstemon

The penstemons, also known as the beard-tongues, are another great American family of plants that have contributed many beautiful plants for our gardens. The spectacular border penstemons, with their spikes of large, brilliantly colored flowers, have been developed from wild species. Lovely as they are, they are not admired by all, and most of them certainly are not candidates for the trough garden.

This wonderful genus has at least one representative in practically every geographic location. It ranges from Alaska to Guatemala. Visit them in their natural haunts in the western mountains and the Great Basin, and be overwhelmed by the number and diversity of the species you will encounter: from tall stately roadside specimens to tiny alpine species, all with lovely colored flowers. Some of the alpine species have startling ice-blue or gentian-blue flowers. Botanists differ in the count of species that exist, but it is over 250 species at least. Classification is very difficult, as the species seems to be evolving still. Nonetheless, penstemons are easily recognized by the long tubular corolla with its five lobes and two-lipped flowers. The name is derived from the Greek and refers to five stamens. *Pente* means five and *stemon*, stamen, which comes as no surprise.

Flower colors include shades of pink, red, violet, all of the blues, plus white; some of the whites can have tinges of yellow.

Penstemons are to be found in our deserts, prairies, open screes, and in the mountains, nearly always in full sun. They fall into two main groups: the herbs, which are soft, having no woody stem, and the woody, shrubby types. They are summer flowering plants in their natural habitat but in gardens some varieties and species can be earlier, blooming in late April and May.

With all these species growing wild around us, it is a shame that too few have been domesticated and are available from nurseries. There are gardeners who grow some of the choice dwarf species from the wild: some are rock gardeners, others wildflower growers.

When it comes to penstemons for the trough garden, there is little choice because many species grow too large. There are choice little species from the western mountains that a few experts grow, mainly from wild-collected seed from seed exchanges. They are far from easy to obtain and not reliable in a wide range of climates, so we rely on what is available from the nurseries.

Let us start with *P. hirsutus*, a popular species from the East Coast, found in fields and woodlands, from Quebec down to Kentucky. This one can grow up to three feet, but, luckily, there is a dwarf form that is firmly established in our gardens, called *P. hirsutus* 'Pygmaeus'. This little plant can vary in height from two inches up to, maybe, four inches. It makes tufts of fairly broad leaves that can have shades of red or purple in them. This coloration intensifies with the onset of winter. The many tubular flowers are carried on very hairy stems (hence the name) and are about three quarters of an inch long. The flowers are a shade of lavender, some say violet, with a white throat and white lips. The plant is hardy and enjoys a little shade during the hot months. Normal trough soil is all it requires, and the same soil moisture as other plants in the trough.

P. rupicola is a westerner found in the Cascade Mountains, continuing through Oregon to Northern California. In the Columbia Gorge it comes down to lower elevations. It is a crevice-dwelling species and may be found hanging from vertical crevices, but seems just as content in horizontal crevices in bold rock outcrops. Once you see it in its natural habitat you will be infatuated with it and not satisfied until you have it growing in your trough.

But you may have to settle for it in a rock garden. It is not happy in a few inches of dusty soil for it must get the roots down to at least a meager supply of moisture. It is a sunlover and lives in fairly dry country, so it does not like a wet climate.

Even when not in flower, the low shrubby habit is attractive with the light blue-gray sheen of the rounded leaves. The flowers are produced in two's or three's on very short stems. In the garden they will start to flower from late April into May. One expert describes the colors as cerise and fuchsia-purple.

Left, *Penstemon rupicola* (p. 90).

Below, with yellow flowers, *Draba rigida* (p.77).

a

Photographs by Rex Murfitt

Above left, small round trough made by Roberta Berg (p. 43). Right, *Dianthus* 'La Bourbouille' (p. 86). Below, *Gentiana sino-ornata* and *G. s. alba* (p. 87). First photo by Joyce Fingerut, others by Rex Murfitt.

Saxifrage 'Rex' in the Section Ligulatae (p. 101).

Anacyclus depressus.

g

Photographs by Rex Murfitt

Acantholimon makes a
tidy bun perched above
rocky terrain (left), while
sedums and succulents fill
in the crevices (center).
Below, the charm of an
aged trough in a terraced
landscape. See pp. 131 to
142 for landscaping
suggestions.

Rex Murfitt

Rex Murfitt

Joyce Fingerut

Others prefer to use "rich red" and "rich pink" to describe the colors. There is a lavender colored variation. Then there is also the pure white form.

A few years ago I planted a 24- by 18-inch trough with six distinct named forms of *P. rupicola*, in the crevices between stones, half buried in the compost, hoping they would grow into bushy mat, flowing over the sides of the trough. They were not happy: whether we had a wetter than usual winter or they were starved I do not know. They needed constant attention to remove dead and untidy growth. The glorious show of color lasted for such a short time and the rest of the year they struggled to stay green and healthy. Moral: plant only one per trough and allow enough of a root run. The species is considered hardy to zone 4. Its survival is more a matter of receiving a little shade and not suffering copious amounts of water.

The following cultivars of *P. rupicola* are usually available from western mailorder nurseries.

P. r. 'Fiddler Mountain' was discovered on the mountain of the same name in the Siskiyous. This form has particularly silvery foliage and rich red flowers.

P. r. 'Diamond Lake' is named for a popular holiday spot in the southern Cascade Mountains. I have been fortunate to have been shown this form in its native home by one of its discoverers. It has rich pink flowers.

P. r. 'Myrtle' is a dwarf form with lavender flowers.

P. r. 'White Knight' or 'Albus'. Either name is used. The white flowers show off the gray-green of the foliage.

P. davidsonii is similar in habit except that the foliage tends to be on the green side rather than the glaucous color of *P. rupicola*. The flower colors are lavender-blue or lavender-purple, but pink forms exist. This species has a wide distribution and, as a result, several forms and variations are known. The differences are botanical, often subtle. Plants purchased from nurseries can be even more variable due to hybrid blood. With the exception of a very dwarf form, sometimes listed as *P. davisonii* var. *menziesii* 'Microphyllus', this species is too large for all but the largest trough. This dwarf form has tiny rounded leaves and forms a low flat mat and violet-blue flowers.

More small species growing wild throughout the west may be suitable to trough gardening, and a few are proving to be useful to gardeners in the warmer, drier states. However, the only way to try them is from seed and experiment with them yourself.

Joyce Fingerut

Phlox

It is unfortunate that a group of American plants that has contributed so much to the garden world offers only a few plants for the trough garden. North America has provided many families and genera of beautiful plants, and *Phlox* rates highly among them.

The genus contains the brightly colored annual *Phlox drummondii*, several tall herbaceous perennial border types, and the colorful mats of the *P. subulata* hybrids, popularly referred to as rock phlox or creeping phlox.

Over a hundred years ago, phlox were finding their way to Europe, and since then they have been hybridized into bright, colorful varieties that have found their way back to us. All the lovely phlox that grow throughout the Eastern woodlands, including the *P. subulata* varieties, are far too boisterous for the average trough garden.

But there are rare, delightful and challenging species from the western mountains of North America. Today in Europe, the demand for these little moss-like cushions is as strong as ever. The challenge to master their cultivation is highly rewarding, with rock gardeners vying with one another to showcase their skills. The thrill of trying to succeed with them is shared just as enthusiastically in North America. They would be ideal if only they were a little easier to grow (but not too easy). People should refrain from digging up these plants in the wild, as seeds are available from reliable suppliers.

Fortunately the transatlantic flow of native phlox has produced a small race of valuable hybrids similar to the subulata hybrids. They were named as a group, *Phlox* x *douglasii*. These plants may have a drop of the western mountain species blood in them, but not enough to render them difficult to grow. Although the whole plant grows to only half the size of the *P. subulata,* the flowers remain the same size and are just as bright and plentiful. Flowering time in most areas is April and May, sometimes lasting into June. Eventually they will become too untidy for the small trough and will have to be replaced or divided. Their demands are few, requiring only the well-drained soil of a sunny trough. After flowering, the dead flowers should be removed, and the plants trimmed lightly.

Following are a few cultivars of *P.* x *douglasii* that may be available from the specialist nurseries. Additional ones may be found described in European nursery lists.

P. x *d.* 'Boothman's Variety', a neat plant, having rounded, lavender colored flowers, with a circle of purple at the center of the flower. This plant was introduced by Stuart Boothman, the owner of Nightingale Nursery at Maidenhead, England, a mecca for alpine plant lovers for many years.

P. x *d.* 'Crackerjack', a brilliant crimson-red flower with dark green foliage, may not be everyone's choice. It cascaded from my trough for three years before removal was necessary due to vigorous growth.

P. x *d.* 'Eva' has a pink flower with a deep crimson eye.

P. x *d.* 'Rosea' or 'Rose Queen' is the lowest-growing variety, although it is vigorous. Stuart Boothman describes the color as silver-pink.

P. x *d.* 'Snow Queen' has a pure white flower with no markings.

Whenever you see *P.* x *douglasii* varieties listed, it is safe to buy one, even if the name does not match the color.

Potentilla

The potentillas are a very large genus of plants that, for the most part, are easy to grow and flower in profusion, although they tend to be difficult along the East Coast and other low, warm, humid regions. They may be found as either herbaceous plants or shrubs, over the Northern temperate regions, from sea level to the mountain tops. They are generally sunlovers and provide treasures are among the earliest rock plants to bloom; neither cold, wind, ice nor snow will daunt them for long, as damaged flowers are soon replaced by emerging new ones.

These dainty harbingers of spring, after the long winter, provide a welcome appearance of bright yellow, pink or white flowers glistening against the silvery domes of the plants. Few can resist the display they present. They are valued, as well, for their neat, compact habit and slow rate of growth: year by year slowly increasing into tight, iron-hard domes of green or silver foliage. Given adequate space at planting time, they require nothing more than to be left alone to gradually fill the crevices and expand over the stones, eventually producing that Old World air so desirable in a trough garden.

Cushion saxes growing in tufa: National Collection, Waterperry, England.

When confronted with a list of *Kabschia* saxifrages (a subsection of *Porphyrion*), it is extremely difficult to make a selection. One reason to reject a variety may be for potential growth habit: a fast-growing variety soon dominates the small landscape. All good catalogs and lists should indicate the ultimate height and spread of each variety described. Descriptive expressions used can give an indication of ultimate size; look for terms such as hard domes, mounds, condensed, and tight cushions. Flower color could be another method of making a choice, but do not let personal bias lead you to reject a plant by reason of its color alone. It is extremely difficult to assess a color until you have seen it in bloom; even color pictures can be misleading.

It is difficult to go wrong if you start with the older tried-and-true plants, such as *S. x irvingii*, with its lovely soft pink, stemless flowers perched on the silvery mat of foliage. *S. x angelica* 'Cranbourne' is another excellent pink cultivar, proven over the years; in this plant, the flowers are carried on short stems over a mound of silver edged, gray-green leaves that are broader and less needlelike than the previous plant. For contrast, try *S. x edithae*, with its delicate shell-pink, slightly cup-shaped flowers, several to a stem. The silvery rosettes are slightly larger than many cushion saxifrages, adding welcome variety to the planting.

There is a wide range of yellow-flowered varieties to consider, from palest moonlight lemon to the deepest of yellows. Some of the oldest and most reliable plants are to found among the yellow cultivars. Check very carefully when making your selection, as many will be too large. Any cultivars listed in association with the name of *S. x boydii*, (a very old hybrid that dates back to 1890), such as 'Aretiastrum' (pictured on page 97), 'Faldonside' or 'Hindhead Seedling', as well as the species itself, will be excellent plants with differing shades of yellow flowers on short stems and neat tidy habit. The foliage will be green or silver-gray. *S. x elizabethae* 'Boston Spa' is another good cultivar to

Rex Murfitt

Saxifraga. x elizabethae 'Boston Spa'

grow in the trough, where it will slowly make a mat six inches across, producing two or three primrose-yellow flowers per stem.

Among the white-flowered types are several quite old varieties that are still as good today as they ever were. In older books, they can be found listed as cultivars of *S. burseriana*. There are a number of admirable plants, such as Ss. 'Brookside', 'Crenata', 'Gloria', 'His Majesty', 'Minor' and 'Princess', to name but a few. All have white flowers with subtle differences in the size of flower or shape of petal. They present a striking picture of large, pristine flowers, yellow centers, red stems and silver mounds of spiky leaves.

S. marginata and its variety *rocheliana* are also welcome additions. Unlike many of the cushion saxifrages, they are natural species, wild plants from the southern mountains of Europe. The leaves have a character of their own: neither needle-like or rounded, they are narrowly elliptical, somewhat eggshaped, or as the botanist would prefer to say, obovate. The plant makes a fine, hard dome of silver-gray that is completely hidden under a mass of snow-white, broadly funnel-shaped flowers, with four or five florets on each two inch stem. The variety *S. m. rocheliana* is very similar, except that the white flowers may be a little more cup shaped.

fun. Some are short and thick, others are long and threadlike, and some yield masses of long runners that cover a lot of surface. *S. ossetiense*, from the Caucasus, has very stout stolons at least six inches long; while *S. montanum*, from Europe, has long, thin, leafy stolons that will soon form a dense mat, quickly causing a problem in the confines of a trough garden.

Of medium-sized rosettes are three species worthy of special mention. They have been removed from the genus *Sempervivum* and placed in the genus *Jovibarba*, this being a change in classification made by botanists. They have been put into a different genus based on the arrangement of their flower parts. Readers will run into ambiguity with plant names in books and catalogs. Remember, when looking through lists, to check under the name *Jovibarba* or some good plants could be overlooked.

Jovibarba arenaria, or *Sempervivum arenarium*, as it was once named, is a case in point. It is one of the smallest species, with rosettes about one-quarter to three-quarters of an inch across. The tiny leaves are tightly incurved, forming tiny balls of bright green which, when grown in sunshine, develop bright red tips to the leaves. *J. sobolifera*, or *S. soboliferum*, while similar in color, has rosettes that are more globular, the tightly closed leaves clasping the rosette. It will have lots of red and coppery coloring. This species is the one that was first called hen and chickens. If there is a need for a big, bold, brightly colored species, then *J. hirta* (*S. hirtum*) is the one. It will stand out noticeably, with its conspicuous, two-inch rosettes of bright green generously colored with shades of red, brown and scarlet.

Among would-be aristocrats of the genus, the cobweb houseleek, *S. arachnoideum,* is a top contender. It owes its name to the cobweb of fine hairs that are drawn from leaf tip to leaf tip, forming an almost solid white mass. Its rosettes are small enough for troughs, about one inch across depending upon soil conditions. The foliage has color—red shades as rule—and this, contrasting with the stark white of the cobwebs, makes for a great plant. In addition, the fact that this species has the nicest flowers of the genus makes it one of the best. The flowers are large for the size of the plant, wide open, starlike and of a bright rose red. There is a dwarf form, *S. a.* 'Minor', with the smallest of rosettes, about a quarter of an inch across, which is ideal for any trough. If you encounter plants with the names of *S. a.* 'Laggeri', 'Tomentosum' and 'Stansfieldii'; do not pass them up, as the opportunity to obtain these attractive forms does not happen every day.

Left, *Sempervivum octopodes*; right, *S. arachnoideum*. Photos by Rex Murfitt.

Other tiny forms are happy in my troughs, are very well behaved and do not take over. One is *S. pumilum* which has rosettes that average less than half an inch, although good growing conditions may increase the mature rosettes to three-quarters of an inch. The flower color is not among the brightest shades, being closer to the purple-brown tones. But the whole is enlivened by a bright green center and upon close inspection, there is a brightness about the plant supplied by the tiny hairs along the leaf margins. It is a clump-forming species, growing into a low, tight group of rosettes which will increase well in the crevices between the sides of the trough and rocks used in the landscape. If you are lucky enough to have soft porous rocks (like real tufa), they will grow on the rock itself, if they have been planted in holes drilled into the soft rock.

Rex Murfitt

Sempervivum ciliosum 'Ali Butusch'

At the top of my list of favorites is *S. ciliosum,* along with its varieties and cultivars. The group originates in the mountains of Bulgaria, the former Yugoslavia and the Greek mountains. They will be found in catalogs listed as *S. ciliosum* (which is the type species) and geographic forms, which will be listed as *S. ciliosum* 'Borisii', *S. c.* 'Mali Hat' and the striking *S. c.* 'Ali Butusch'. 'Borisii' is named for one of the local kings and the latter two after the mountains on which they were found. They are all bright gray globes with incurving, red-backed leaves, perching on the soil. Much of their bright appearance stems from the masses of long white hairs that cover the rosettes. The stolons that carry the offsets are numerous and look extremely handsome with the little round offsets on the ends. It may be necessary to thin out some of the stolons, which are then easily rooted, providing a supply of young plants for replacements and gifts.

To this point, emphasis has been on the smaller sorts of sempervivums, but this does not mean that the larger kinds with rosettes of two inches or more need be ignored. There are many fine specimens among them, and nothing is more attractive than a trough planted exclusively to a mixture of sempervivums, both the large and the small.

S. tectorum is the commonest and most easily recognized of the genus, all too often found growing on both sunny and shady walls. It is a common sight in many urban gardens, where it survives uncared for and uncomplaining and looking very unattractive; more often than not, the rosettes are fat, soft, dull green and the leaves are wide open, destroying any character the plant might have had. But if *S. tectorum* and some of its forms are grown as an alpine should be, they are among the most dramatic plants in the genus. The rosettes are neat, somewhat flattened, and a lovely bluish-gray with a contrasting purple-crimson tip on every leaf. They will make a compact mat of closely packed rosettes, from which the short stout stolons bear the offsets. This group will require removal of the unsightly spent flower stems: an operation that will temporarily leave holes in the perfection of the mat. Similarly, the stolons will need some thinning out to make space for the young offsets (some of which can be used to fill in the holes); otherwise, they will establish themselves on top of the plant, spoiling its shape. When hunting for *S. tectorum* and its cultivars in the nursery lists, be sure to look under the name *S. calcareum* as well as *S. tectorum* because they may be listed under either name. The names to look for are *Ss. alpinum*, 'Mrs. Giuseppi', and 'Sunset', which, as the name implies, is a lovely form that assumes orange-red tints in the fall.

All of the sempervivums are fun. Although it is true they do not supply much in the way of colorful flowers, for year-round appeal they always contribute something to catch the eye, even in the worst weather; and they are easy to grow.

BULBOUS PLANTS FOR TROUGHS

Plants from bulbs (including bulblike structures such as corms and tubers) can look sensational in troughs, but they present challenges. Bulbs need moisture in spring, like most other plants. But in summer they aestivate (go dormant) and need to be kept dry to help keep them from rotting. However, the roots may still appreciate occasional moisture; they do not prosper with the hot, arid "baking" that is sometimes recommended.

So, where to place them? With the usual herbaceous plants, for their springtime watering, or with succulents, which tolerate summer's dry spells? Or simply in a trough of their own, which will eventually look rather boring, once flowering is over and the foliage is dead or, worse, dying. Foliage of bulbs, even of the petite types suited for troughs, eventually becomes a problem. When fresh, it is fine; while departing (yellowing and withering slowly), it is a liablity; and once gone, it leaves a gap—or an opportunity.

One solution is to grow bulbs in small pots which may be added to a trough as the bulbs come into bloom, and removed once the show is over. The foliage can then ripen elsewhere, out of sight.

This gap can be filled with small-scale annual or tender plants, preferably started in the same size pot. A good example is *Silene pendula*, a dwarf, weeping catchfly with bright pink flowers. A plant of suitable scale for the larger trough is *Dianthus barbatus*, the familiar sweet william. Look for the short-stemmed forms. Garden centers abound with these fragrant flowers in striking shades of pink, purple, red and white, sometimes in combination. Choose the dwarfest cultivars, suitable at about six inches tall, but avoid taller cultivars which reach almost two feet.

For a more subtle tone, choose *Helichrysum petiolatum* 'Limelight' solely for its foliage. Interesting and refined, the fuzzy round leaves of a soft chartreuse-gray gradually fill in the branching arms that will spill over the sides of the trough all summer, until the first hard frost. Pinch back tips to keep it from becoming too tall or lank.

With the pot-swapping plan in mind, choose bulbs with proportions that work in a trough. The common bulbous genera, *Allium, Crocus, Narcissus, and Tulipa*, all contain fine hardy dwarf species.

To preserve all these pristine miniature blooms from the early season's mud splatters, mulch them well with clean, rough (unsandy) grit.

The usual bulb-growing advice pertains: the medium must be well-drained, or the succulent bulbs will surely rot. Beyond that, how you handle their year-round cycle in your troughs is a matter of personal taste.

Allium

Garden alliums (onions) offer several species for troughs. One with uncommonly attractive foliage is *A. senescens glaucum*. Though technically classified as a bulb, there is not the usual problem with dying leaves. This attractive foliage appears in late spring and remains to see the garden season out. The scythe-shaped leaves, flat and pale grey-blue, swirl into clusters. The small lilac globes, on three- to four-inch stems, appear late in the garden season—reason enough to grow this plant. A delicate and possibly more elusive onion is our native *A. perdulce*. Its very fine foliage and rich pink, graceful, spring-blooming flowers make it worth the extra effort to locate. Seeds may be offered through rock garden and native plant societies' seed exchanges.

Crocus

When purchasing crocuses for the trough, favor the early species over the later-blooming, larger hybrid cultivars. Species such as *Cc. chrysanthus, sieberi* and *tommasinianus* offer the range of traditional crocus colors: white, mauve to icy blue, and cheery yellow, in the requisite trough-sized plant. This genus offers an uncommon bonus in its fall-blooming species. *Cc. speciosus, kotschyanus* and the slightly more tender (zone 7) *goulimyi* all bloom with a rich, warm pinky lilac deep into autumn. For a creamy-white flower, search out *C. niveus* or *C. ochroleucus*. Bulb suppliers are offering these once-rare corms with increasing frequency and, fortunately, decreasing prices.

Early blooms of *Cyclamen coum*.

Cyclamen

Several species of *Cyclamen* are excellent candidates for trough gardens. These plants, grown from tubers, carry remarkable ornamental interest for most of the year: the period of dormancy is short or, in the case of *C. purpurascens*, non-existent. The standard rose-magenta color of cyclamen flowers could be considered garish, were it not for the exquisitely graceful flower form. The leaves-shapely, substantial and often beautifully marked with silver and white—provide a long season of interest. Lately, several new forms have appeared with leaves entirely of silver or pewter.

C. hederifolium is surprisingly hardy for a plant of mostly Mediterranean distribution, surviving temperatures down to -10 degrees F in the garden, though it may be more tender in a container. *Cc. coum, repandum* and *purpurascens* are a little less hardy, wanting either a climate one zone milder or greater winter protection. Each of the species varies in the timing of the appearance of its flowers and leaves, so that careful selection can keep the trough interesting for as long as there is someone outside to enjoy it.

They require the same cultural conditions: first, very well drained soil: continued wetness, winter or summer, is anathema to the succulent tubers. Then, they will benefit from good bright light, but not direct sunlight, not even in winter. They enjoy companion plants, and look at home in a woodland setting. They are not bothered by root competition from other plants, including foraging woody plants, but do resent disturbance of their own roots by the gardener's digging and transplanting.

The dainty dwarf forms lately appearing in florist shops and supermarkets are not hardy, but can be used as long-lasting annuals, especially during cool weather, either to be replaced annually or protected elsewhere over the winter and dropped back into place each spring.

Narcissus

Some of the tiniest daffodils, *N. minor* and *N. asturiensis*, are also the earliest—and the toughest. They have to be, blooming as they do in the midst of some of the worst early spring weather. These two have the classic daffodil cup-and-perianth form, though greatly reduced in size to less than an inch. An interesting variation in form is *N. bulbocodium*, the hoop petticoat daffodil, where there is virtually no perianth, but the cup (corona) enlarges to form a funnel-shaped tube: very showy for its one-inch size.

Tulipa

There are a few species tulips small enough to look at home in a trough. Again, the earliest are the smallest. *T. humilis, pulchella and violacea* may

Jane Grushow

have been sorted out to the satisfaction of the botanists, but this news has had no effect upon most of the bulb tradesmen. So purchase any of the above, and feel reasonably certain that you will be growing an early-blooming, dwarf (four- to six-inch) tulip, in varying shades of lavender to violet (all of them lovely) with a central blotch that may be yellow (in the true *T. humilis*) or an interesting navy blue. You will enjoy it, whatever the name.

Tulipa tarda

WOODY PLANTS

Trees for the Trough Garden

Dwarf trees and shrubs are useful for providing a feeling of realism to the miniature landscape. They help set the scale by giving an impression of height and depth, or distance. There is always a risk that a trough landscape can look flat and lacking in contours and movement. An example of their value can be demonstrated by planting a tiny dwarf juniper to represent a magnificent forest giant.

Select a dwarf that has an outline similar to the taller tree. The Noah's Ark juniper, *Juniperus communis* 'Compressa', is ideally suited for this role. A high cliff can be suggested by planting a Noah's Ark juniper close to the base of one of the rocks in the trough landscape; this immediately sets a scale that transforms both tree and stone into a lifelike model of a real scene.

Similarly, a mountainside or a woodland glade is suggested by grouping several upright trees in a random and informal planting. If the plants can be of differing heights and age, the scene will be far more convincing. To be authentic, place the forests at the lowest part of the mountains, where they belong, so that the mountain rises from the forest.

By utilizing natural differences in shape and habit of the different types of dwarf trees, it is possible to develop ideas. As the slender, upright form represents a forest tree, others can be used to portray other alpine settings. There are trees that are mounded, or broader than tall, or flat-topped, with no dominant leader. There are also forms that virtually creep along the ground.

A hike up a mountainside, anywhere in the world, will quickly provide ideas that we should try to imitate. As the ascent progresses, the forest trees gradually give way to those of a different stature: their crowns have fewer and shorter branches. Eventually the trees are thinner, and farther apart, with graceful pendant branches, shaped to help shed the heavy falls of snow. Here, unlike the trees of the forest with their bold clear trunks, branches grow all the way down the trunk to the ground, often spreading around the base of the tree as gracefully as a long skirt.

Higher and closer to the timberline, the trees become low, contorted specimens, shaped by continued exposure to strong winds and harsh winters. Wonderful mounded or sprawling trees are produced by these conditions, each specimen a work of art and an inspiration to alpine gardener and bonsai grower alike. Finally, up near the summit slopes, the few trees to be found are reduced to low, ground-hugging mats, hiding from the wind in what little protection they can find.

Using these observations and selecting the appropriate dwarf trees, imaginative Lilliputian landscapes can be designed. Do not yield to the temptation to plant a bold upright tree, like a sentinel on the highest point of the mountain. This is often done and it may be fun, but is totally unnatural.

The task of choosing and buying dwarf coniferous trees for the trough is easier with some first-hand knowledge; but failing this, a visit to a good collection of dwarf conifers makes it is possible to see actual plants growing. Reference books, particularly if they contain quality photographs, will also assist in an understanding of the scope and habits of these plants.

Rex Murfitt

Here, dwarf evergreens and tightly mounded rock garden plants find shelter against the "mountain peak."

The list from a reliable nursery can describe in detail what a plant is expected to do. More helpful still, the plants are sometimes listed in groups according to ultimate size and spread. Be prepared to find that the very choicest cultivars will be in short supply, particularly the slowest-growing dwarfs. By their very nature, it will take several years to produce a saleable plant. Choose only those plants with the smallest of needles, and with branches that are close together, not widely spaced on the stem. Look for a balance and harmony between the size of the leaves and the size of the tree: do they seem proportionate? Large leaves do not look convincing on a small plant; especially one that is supposed to portray a wind-riven alpine dwarf. Be particularly careful when considering the pines; many of them have a bad habit of rapidly dominating a small landscape. It is very easy to be captivated by a young specimen, only to have it quickly outgrow its allotted space.

In this section, the emphasis is on coniferous species, perhaps giving the impression that there are no other appropriate types. Of course, this is not the case. There are a few deciduous trees and even a few broad-leaved evergreen trees that we can consider. Providing it is not overdone, it is possible to mix them together, as well as leave room for some flowering plants.

Abies

There is a choice little balsam fir which is extremely useful in alpine landscape schemes, as it has some of the characteristics of the real alpine firs of the very high elevations. The plant's proper botanical name may be a little confusing sometimes, as it seems to have several names. Currently, it is listed as *Abies balsamea f. hudsonia*, or it may be named *A. hudsonica*. Occasionally the name *'Nana'* is added, and hopefully this really means dwarf. As long as one of these combinations of names is present, it is a safe bet that you have the right plant. It is a dwarf, slow-growing tree, shaped like the flat-topped specimens seen among the rocks. It has many gnarled branches, and its leaves are an attractive glossy, dark green, with the bright silvery undersides typical of the genus. The three terminal buds are mid-brown and slightly waxy. The whole plant is reminiscent of the balsam fir of the North Woods, even to the aroma. While it may not be a spectacular plant, it does have its own unique appearance that suggests those alpine trees kept low by wind and weather. It is quite happy in a trough garden and seems to slow its growth rate to suit the soil and space available. Any errant twigs that might shoot up, full of vigor, may be pruned back to a lower branch, keeping the plant compact.

Rex Murfitt

Dwarf balsam fir, the main feature of this trough, contrasts well with saxifrages in bloom.

Chamaecyparis

Chamaecyparis, or false cypress, is a genus that contains many forest-sized trees. On this continent we have the Port Orford cedar, *C. lawsoniana* from Oregon and northern California and the yellow cedar, *C. nootkatensis* of the Northwest Coast. There are two Japanese species: the popular Hinoki cypress, *C. obtusa,* and the lesser-known Sawara cypress, *C. pisifera.*

There is some confusion because some are commonly called cypress, while others are called cedar, when in actual fact thay are all in the same genus. These inconsistencies are mainly the result of years of use by gardeners. At one time, the *Chamaecyparis* were ranked in the same genus as the cypresses, so it is hardly surprising there was, and still is, some confusion. The familiar red cedar of the eastern United States is really a juniper, *Juniperus virginiana,* and not a cedar at all.

It is remarkable that trees capable of growing to a hundred and fifty feet or more are able to produce some of the most desirable of all the dwarf conifers. The Hinoki cypress, *C. obtusa,* has produced so many different dwarf cultivars that selecting a particular one is difficult indeed. To compound matters, they are renowned for the confused state of their names. Many of them undoubtedly grow too large for the trough, however there are plenty of different cultivars from which we may choose. Some are the smallest, most compact and slow-growing of all the dwarf conifers in cultivation. It is in this group that we find the miniature, domelike, compact bush, sometimes referred to as the tennis-ball cypress. This is an apt description, giving a clear picture of the style of the plant.

Chamaecyparis obtusa 'Nana Gracilis'

Those who recall the foliage of the cedar tree will have a mental image of the foliage of the *C. obtusa* group. The foliage is usually a dark, rich green and the branches are spread out in flat, fan-shaped tiers, with each tiny scale-like leaf tightly appressed to the stem (lying flat against the stem). Probably the finest selection is *C. obtusa* 'Caespitosa', a dense bun of dark green, tightly appressed foliage. It is extremely slow-growing, taking many years to produce enough growth to make a specimen a few inches across and as high.

The next few varieties are grouped roughly by size and similarity of shape. They are all wonderful plants, each with its own character, but with subtle differences difficult to describe. I would be happy with any of them. *C. obtusa* 'Juniperoides' is akin to 'Caespitosa' except that it is not so tightly congested and the branch tips have a slightly weeping habit. The whole plant has a more airy and open appearance; perhaps informal might be the right word. *C. Juniperoides compacta* is dwarfer still. Another cultivar, offered under the name *C. obtusa* 'Minima', is a plant with a different arrangement of the branches: they are more erect, pushing upward.

Pick up any current catalog of dwarf conifers and you will find that some of the plants described here will be offered. Continue reading through the *C. obtusa* section and you will arrive at the *C. obtusa* 'Nana' listings; depending on the list, there could be up to a dozen different cultivars described. This group is the most popular of the whole genus; it is the dwarf Hinoki cypress of popular gardening and almost every garden center will offer at least two or three varieties. I can only offer this advice: they may very well grow too quickly and too large. They are generally broadly conical, the branches are usually fan-shaped but this can vary from being flat, sometimes drooping at the tip, to rolled, to an almost cup shape. In addition, the foliage color will

117

range from an extremely dark green, through various lighter shades of green, to golden-yellow and bronze.

In favored climates, some are known to have attained the height of several feet, so they are not quite the dwarfest forms. However, there is one clone of *C. obtusa* 'Nana' which is rare and very dwarf and slow growing. Its foliage is almost a black-green and rolled into a cup shape. Should you see the "true form" advertised, buy it even if not for the trough. Once again I offer the advice: go to a nursery and see for yourself; at least you will have some idea of what is available and be armed with a few names to start the ball rolling.

Now comes the bad news. Many of these *Chamaecyparis* forms are not considered hardy in all areas. Often it is more a problem with dessicating winds than with out-and-out cold. If some protection can be provided, it will lessen damage of this nature. Summer, too, contributes its share of problems: hot afternoon sun will scorch tender foliage and hot, drying winds will cause similar damage. Therefore, if these plants are to be used, the trough should be located with a degree of shade and wind protection.

These notes so far have emphasized only the smallest varieties of dwarf conifers, with the aim of introducing them and dispelling some of the confusion surrounding them. At the same time, you may have been given the impression that only tiny trees are acceptable. This is not the case; the gardener must make that decision, based upon the size of the container and the garden design in mind. Naturally, the larger the container, the greater the room for a larger tree. Some of my trough gardens have trees that are two feet high, rather more columnar than spreading, as they will take up less of the available

Jane Grushow

space. There is no doubt that a few tall specimens will add enormously to the overall effect of a group of trough gardens by providing substance and height to a planting that could otherwise lack vertical features.

One tree per trough is usually sufficient because as it grows it demands more space. Valuable space can be saved by planting a tree as far into one of the corners as the root ball will allow; then the branches will grow by expanding over the sides of the trough rather than covering the valuable planting space of the trough surface.

Juniperus

Juniperus communis 'Compressa' has long been a favorite of trough gardeners, mainly because it can be relied upon to remain a dwarf. As the the years go by, the rate of growth slows down and the gray needles become more and more congested. The plant has strong appeal

This upright dwarf juniper (right) punctuates Rex Murfitt's line of troughs.

118

because it is a perfect juniper tree in miniature; its outline is best described as the shape of a candle flame.

Strictly speaking, *J. communis* 'Hibernica' hardly qualifies as an alpine plant, as it is closely related to the Irish juniper. The upright habit is much like the formal lines of a cypress in a Mediterranean landscape. Nonetheless, it is extremely effective in the small-scale garden, even if it may not be a true dwarf. I have a forty year-old specimen in the rock garden that is now four feet high; while in one of the troughs, a 20-year-old specimen is only a few inches over two feet. It is a columnar plant, with compressed branches ascending steeply. The tiny needles are about a quarter of an inch long and are quite prickly. They clothe the tree in such numbers that no branches are visible, giving an overall pleasing gray-green color. Many illustrations are found in gardening books that prove its popularity and acceptance by the most accomplished alpine gardeners.

One of these gardeners, Mr. R. S. Corley, commented in an Alpine Garden Society Bulletin in England, some years ago, that "It is seldom made use of as it should be, that is, planted in groups." He then describes how several plants of differing sizes should be grouped: "One large specimen and three or more smaller ones placed close together, with another smaller one a little apart from the rest." He paints such a clear picture that the desire to go out and create such a planting is overwhelming.

Now a few words of warning: cold, dry winter winds will sometimes kill a few branches, eventually turning them red-brown. The extent of the kill can then be seen and this dead wood can be pruned out. Providing the damage is limited, new growth soon covers the scars. In some areas of the country, webworms and some mites attack the foliage, causing ugly brown patches of dead leaves. These are extremely unpleasant pests that can ruin a valuable plant. If caught in time, it is possible to eradicate pests by spraying and by washing all the debris away. Feeding may encourage new shoots and leaves. It is vital to inspect the plants regularly for early signs of infestation, making it easier to control the pests before too much damage has occurred. Frequent mistings with water during hot, dry weather is a great deterrent.

Picea

The spruce trees are as common in the mountains as the balsam firs, usually growing in each other's company. Many different species are found worldwide, from sea level to the mountains. The Norway spruce from Europe is well known in our gardens; the same can be said of the Colorado spruce, particularly the famous blue varieties. Embarking on discussion of the dwarf forms of the spruces is comparable to a journey that has no end in sight; the Norway spruce alone must have dozens and dozens of dwarf forms.

Dwarf, that is, in relation to the normal forest-tree size; whether they are dwarf enough for the trough garden is another story. With so many differing yet similar varieties available today, confusion and errors are bound to occur. Once again, the only sure way of knowing the plant you have purchased is exactly the one you wish to acquire, is by hand-picking it yourself at the nursery, wherever that is possible. On the other hand, if you are prepared to try a plant on its face value, be prepared to transplant it out of the trough if it shows signs of becoming too large. Give it a fair trial, for sometimes the constraints of the trough will keep it small.

The dwarf forms of the Norway spruce, *Picea abies*, are much like the balsams in their dwarf forms, as they also keep many of the characteristics of their genus. In particular, the general color and shapes of the leaves and the buds are typically spruce-like, sometimes retaining the sharp prickly needles. Of course they have the same delightful scent as other spruces. Without a doubt, they are an asset to the authentic miniature landscape.

A few of the dwarfer forms have been in cultivation for a great many years, particularly *P. a.* 'Gregoryana' and the similar *P. a.* 'Echiniformis'. The

Rex Murfitt

Like this one in Rex Murfitt's lineup, spruces for troughs should have small needles, densely packed, and an appealing shape.

latter plant has the common name of hedgehog spruce because of its sharp needle points. It is interesting to learn that the name is not taken from the shape of the plant, but from the spiny, prickly nature of the foliage. A slow-growing variety, it is very suitable for the trough as it adds the permanence and character of a spruce tree. It also has a valuable outline, in that it supplies a shape which is a transition between the upright tree shape and the low, flat trees of the timberline. It is a neat, tidy, mounded cushion with little gray-green needles.

P. a. 'Gregoryana' grows into a perfect mound, having very dense dark-green foliage with a touch of gray. The arrangement of the needles makes an interesting feature as they radiate around the tips of the twigs; the central cluster of yellowish buds strongly suggests a bouquet. The leaves are about three-fourths of an inch long and slightly spiny.

P. a. 'Pygmaea' is another variety that has long been in cultivation and, as the name suggests, is suitable for our purposes. It is very slow growing and with age will grow into a cone shape with a very broad base: a squat, pointed tree that is a wonderful replica of an ancient alpine specimen. Its foliage is a pleasant shade of green and the needles are very short, displaying the yellow-gray color of the twigs.

Pinus

There is nothing that adds such a touch of permanence and age to a trough garden as a well-proportioned pine tree, particularly one with a branch structure which shows some intricate patterns. The genus *Pinus* is large group, with species coming from all corners of the globe, along with their many dwarf forms. Dwarf is a relative term in this case, since many are small enough for the average garden but grow far too large for our purposes. There are a few extremely compact forms that are as neat as any other tiny conifer; unfortunately, they are sometimes difficult to obtain. Many of the tree forms grow slowly and remain small for several years before they get into their stride and begin to grow and attain their ultimate height. Life in the restricted growing conditions of the trough will hold back growth for many years, in some cases indefinitely. Should a pine show signs of distress, such as stunted or brown, unsightly needles, or dead and dying branches, it has reached the point when it must be removed and replaced.

The popular mugo pine, *Pinus mugo*, has just about as many combinations to its name as it has variety in its growth habits. It can be found listed as a form of *Pinus montana,* such as *P. m.* 'Mugo', or *P.* 'Mughus'; there is even a combination called *P. m.* 'Mugo Mughus'. Regardless of how it is identified, it will be too big for our trough.

The species originates in the mountains of Europe and is generally considered a dwarf by garden standards, even though some types will grow to a great size. Unless it is possible to obtain guaranteed truly dwarf stock, it is better to avoid the mugo pine itself and try for some of the truly dwarf cultivars that are offered by some nurseries.

The old variety, *P. m.* 'Gnom', is an example. Yes, this is the correct spelling, although I have also seen it listed as 'Gnome'. It is a flat-topped mound of a plant, eventually becoming wider than it is high. In Britain, it is able to attain six feet high—in 50 years, which is no problem to most of us! The branches are quite dense, with dark green needles about an inch long.

There are several other small forms of mugo pine offered under names such as 'Pumilio' and 'Compacta', plus a few others with names that suggest they are dwarf hummocks. Having had no personal experience growing them, it is not possible for me to comment on them.

The Scots pine, *P. sylvestris,* although itself not a small tree, has produced several very pleasant dwarf forms which would be worth investigating. I particularly enjoy *P. sylvestris* 'Beuvronensis', which has a pleasing branch pattern that fits in well with a mountain landscape. The needles are reputed to be about half an inches long, but I am afraid that my plant has longer needles—part of the price of gardening in our mild Northwest climate, where evergreens often continue growing for nine months.

Jane Grushow

Dwarf pine in small trough.

121

Tsuga

The pines may leave the gardener more than a little frustrated for, likeable as they are, they do leave us wanting some of the more diminutive types. This is not so with *Tsuga* (the hemlocks): they offer a wide range of variations in size, habit and even color of foliage. They are among the very few needled evergreens that will thrive in the shade. Furthermore, they are generally available. If I were limited to one group of dwarf conifers for miniature gardening, it would be the Canadian hemlocks.

Rex Murfitt

Tsuga canadensis 'Jeddeloh'

The Eastern or Canadian hemlock, *Tsuga canadensis,* very common throughout the eastern part of North America, is a graceful tree and highly valued as a garden plant, particularly where evergreen trees are not prevalent. In nature it is very variable, especially when grown from seed. This results in a large number of dwarf varieties being introduced, either from past collections in the wild or currently being raised from seed in nurseries and private gardens. The dwarfs are very hardy; most will tolerate a certain amount of sun, while others are happier with some shade. Fortunately, they are not generally prey to the scale problems that can infest the straight species, when it is grown south of its usual range.

Rather than trying to describe every cultivar, it makes sense to give an overall description of the group, then zero in on a few individuals. The hemlocks give the feeling of being gentle plants, with light, airy foliage and thin twigs that elegantly droop at their tips. The needles themselves convey this airy feeling, as they are quite short and thin, well-spaced in two ranks along the twigs. The smaller varieties may be conveniently grouped by habit: there are the low-growing, ground-hugging types; the tree-shaped, upright kinds; and the tiny mounds, domes, buns and irregularly-shaped dwarfs.

T. c. 'Cole', or its older name, 'Cole's Prostrate', lies completely flat on the ground and, as it grows, the branches follow the contours of any stones—cascading over walls and through rock gardens. The center of the plant is almost bare of foliage, displaying the bark and wonderfully intricate branch structure. The area that the mature plant can cover may make its value as a trough plant doubtful: it is capable, over a period of a few years, of covering several square feet. It would make a spectacular addition to a large trough if it could be planted toward the sides and allowed to drape itself down to the ground. Unfortunately, other residents of the trough would likely succumb to the root competition. Should a suitably large container be available, fill it with a good mixture of well-drained soil containing lots of organic matter, place the trough where it will receive some afternoon shade and try one for yourself.

T. c. 'Jervis', or 'Nearing', was discovered in the wild near Port Jervis, New York, by Guy Nearing, a great plantsman and rhododendron breeder from New Jersey. A popular and excellent variety, it has a slow-growing, pyramidal tree shape, with crowded branches in an irregular pattern. The mid-green leaves are heavily clustered on the shoots.

T. c. 'Jeddeloh', contrasting in form to 'Jervis', makes an informal and graceful bush with a flat top. Its branches are horizontal, tiered and drooping at the tips, with foliage a noticeably light green. Although this variety may not symbolize the high alpine landscape, it makes a lovely feature for a trough. Not all troughs need to be alpine, do they? All that is required to create a lovely effect are a couple of rounded stones, to add a little ruggedness to the scene, with the hemlock planted off center, and a couple of alpine plants. A ten year-old plant is still content in one of my troughs

When we come to the very tiny cultivars there is a wide choice. If one dares to generalize, they are little balls with tiny, tiny leaves and congested branches, and are extremely slow growing. I doubt if one could go wrong with any of them. Look for cultivars such as 'Horsford Dwarf', 'Minuta' or 'Pygmaea', For a change, try 'Hussii', one of the slower-growing varieties, with the main branches shooting out at oblique angles, bearing short, stubby branchlets which emphasize the pleasing, open structure of the tree.

Joyce Fingerut

An imaginative planting of dwarf pine in an ancient stone quern.

These selections will provide a few reliable varieties to start a trough garden; from then on, feel free to contemplate some of the other wonderful cultivars available. Be on your guard: dwarf conifers are habit-forming and it is easy to become a collector, ending with all of your troughs full of them.

Rhododendron

When we think of *Rhododendron*, we are likely to think of the large flowering shrubs from the Himalaya or the hybridists' colorful shrubs, which are hardly subjects for the miniature garden. Nevertheless, there exist many dwarf kinds eminently suited to the trough garden. Once more we look to the mountains, where many excellent dwarf species are to be found. Since their earliest introduction to our gardens, a great deal of hybridizing has occurred, by gardeners as well as plant breeders. As a result of their efforts, a range of excellent dwarf plants is now available to us, adding more variety to our trough gardens. These little shrubs have a fascination of their own and it is very easy to become addicted to these durable treasures.

Compact plants with small leaves, thin twiggy branches, and lovely bell-shaped flowers are available in several sizes and shapes. Some of these tough little plants originate from the "roof of the world" to quote Reginald Farrer, one of the famous early plant hunters, who introduced several important species into cultivation. They come from high alpine meadows of the mountains of India, China, Tibet, Burma and the high Himalaya. Here, they clothe the ground, much as heathers do on the high moorlands of Scotland.

The many differing species grow in great carpets, covering the mountainsides and moorlands, often running together into a multicolored patchwork: a magnificent sight when they are in flower.

Actual leaf size of a typical dwarf rhododendron. Those most suited for troughs are even smaller.

When it comes to the garden, these tiny rhododendrons demand the same soil conditions as larger rhododendrons. Primarily, they cannot tolerate soils that contain any lime, or have a pH much above neutral. They require a humusy soil, with an addition of plenty of coarse sand or grit for fast drainage plus the moisture-retentive qualities of peat. Prolonged drought will be fatal. Growing in a shady trough is excellent for them, providing it is not dense shade: the greater the amount of shade, the less they will flower. Although they are equipped to withstand the harsh climate of the Himalayan mountains, these plants will not prosper if exposed to cold, biting, lowland winds.

Where most gardeners measure their plants in feet, the trough gardener must use inches. There are many lovely dwarf rhododendrons that form rounded bushes with masses of small elegant flowers and branches, leaves and flowers all in harmony and scale with one another. Enchanting as they are, many will grow too large for the average-sized trough, even though it may take many years. It is usually a case of proportion that can make or break a landscape. For example, even an attractive rounded miniature rhododendron shrub, full of tiny flowers will look out of balance if it dominates other elements of the miniature landscape. The same principle applies to a tall plant in a shallow container: the proportions will appear unbalanced. Furthermore, the plant will soon exhaust the shallow depth of soil and a poor unhappy plant will result. There are several species and hybrids available in the nurseries that we might consider. However some of them might be difficult to establish and grow; and then there are others that are difficult to obtain.

All of the plants now clustered around the species name of *Rhododendron calostrotum* are trough-worthy shrubs. *R. calostrotum* ssp. *keleticum* is a compact mounding plant with an open branch structure. It has branches that are somewhat prostrate, turning up slightly just at the tips. The dark green, shiny leaves have little hairs along their margins, just like eyelashes! The flowers look like tiny open saucers of a purplish-crimson color, spotted with deeper markings, and the peak of their flowering time occurs in May. It is a tough little plant, growing only to about four- to six-inches high and is an excellent candidate for a trough.

R. calostrotum ssp. *keleticum,* Radicans Group, probably has the smallest species we might choose. It is a mat-forming, creeping plant from the high open moorlands of Tibet. In a trough, it will retain its two- or three inch height and slowly spread its matted stems, which are covered with tiny dark green leaves. Depending upon local climate, the single flowers are produced in May or June, on slender stems that are just long enough to elevate the flowers above the foliage. Each flower is about an inch across, and is flat and open-faced. The color can be purple, violet or pale purple, depending upon the individual clone. Care must be taken to ensure that the soil never dries out, especially during the active growing season.

Jane Grushow

Rhododendron seedling growing in a crack in the boulder.

R. campylogynum is an appealing species, well worth including in a trough. Although it is capable of growing into a 12-inch, bushy hummock, it is unlikely to achieve this height within the confines of a trough. It has tiny, shiny, aromatic leaves carried on spreading branches with short branchlets. It is interesting enough to be grown for the shape of the flowers alone: they are often described as resembling little thimbles nodding their heads on stiff little stems that lift the flowers clear of the plant. Normally the color is a light purple, but there are forms that may be pink or shades of rose. It is well worth shopping for these alternative colors.

R. campylogynum, Myrtilloides Group, offers essentially smaller versions of the preceding species. The branches are erect and reddish-brown; the leaves are spread around the branches and are glossy green on the upper surface and glaucous below—all surfaces attractively spotted with tiny scales. Flowers are solitary on slender stems, plum colored and darkly spotted. The blooms are smaller than the straight species, but retain the waxy appearance.

Rhododendron names are affected by reclassification and change by botanists, as are many other plant names. If you cannot find any of these plants under their current names, purchase plants with any of the names listed above, either singly or in any combination, and you will be assured of a first-class shrub for your trough garden.

R. impeditum should be included in any selection of dwarf rhododendrons as it is a popular species for the smaller garden and usually readily available. It is capable, over a period of many years, of growing into a bush of some two feet high and as much across, although there is little danger of this happening in a trough garden. There, it will form a neat rounded mound, with masses of tiny branchlets and extremely attractive little leaves which give the impression of being silver-gray. This is owing to the leaf coloring, green on top and

Jane Grushow

Rhododendron 'Patty Bee'

gray-green on the underside; the fact that they are also well covered with tiny scales adds to the silvery appearance. Flowers are borne in such prolific clusters that virtually all foliage is obscured. Their color generally is a light, pale purple, but there are forms available that will run to the bluish shades; regardless of the color, the plants always give a light, bright appearance. Flowering time will be April to May. The one drawback to *R. impeditum* is that it will not tolerate heat, and so cannot be grown in the open garden in the southern, or even mid-Atlantic states.

R. fastigiatum is an upright little shrub and, as the name implies, the branches are fastigiate, meaning that they are parallel, erect, clustered branches, in the manner of a Lombardy poplar. These ascendent, light brown, twiggy branchlets bear clustered leaves at their tips. The tiny leaves are oval, gray-green and heavily coated with little scales on the leaf surfaces, as well as on the twigs. Light purple flowers are carried four or five in a truss (cluster), with individual flower stems so short as to be invisible. This helps to clothe the whole plant in color. The flower color is generally a shade of light purple, though there are pink forms as well. Under good conditions, this species will grow to a height of about 18 inches. Over a length of time it might become too large for the smaller trough. It can be used with the understanding that when it gets too big, it will be lifted and replaced.

The dwarf rhododendrons recommended so far all tend to flower in purple and similar colors. Although they are not dull or somber colors, some lighter colors might be appreciated to provide variety. There are several lovely hybrids that will fill the bill nicely.

R. 'Chikor', for example, has bell-shaped, bright lemon-yellow flowers in terminal clusters. It is capable of growing into a compact bush about a foot high. *R.* 'Curlew' might be a few inches taller, but remains a neat, compact, slightly spreading shrub, with small, shiny leaves.

One final plant to consider is the choice little variant of the taller *R. keiskii,* named *R. keiskii* 'Yaku Fairy'. It comes to us from the austere heights of Mt. Kuromi, on the island of Yakushima, which lies off the southernmost tip of Japan. This is a tough, hardy little plant, slowly spreading its prostrate branches so low to the soil that the leaves appear to lie almost flat upon the ground. These leaves, which are about one inch long and half as wide at their widest point, are a matte green, and have a prominent midrib. A well-grown plant will, in late April to May, all but cover itself with creamy yellow flowers, produced in trusses composed of three or four individual florets. With flowers that are quite large for such a small plant, they are usually about one and a half inches across, shaped like wide open bells and beautifully finished with a central group of brown anthers.

There are so many rhododendrons that could be grown in a trough garden it is not practical to list them all. The main problems are that some may be difficult to grow or of doubtful hardiness in some parts of the country and plants may be hard to find in non-specialty nurseries. There would be little value in describing plants that fall into these categories regardless of how worthy they may be. Dwarf rhododendrons are truly fascinating and it is easy to fall under their spell. For further study, there are many excellent works that specialize in dwarf rhododendrons exclusively.

Deciduous Trees and Shrubs

Once any coniferous or evergreen trees have been planted, there may be additional room for a small deciduous shrub, or two. Even where space has allowed only one tree, it still might be desirable to provide an intermediate layer to the height and form of the woody planting.

Sorbus reducta

Not only will this fill in the landscape, it provides further seasonal appeal. Bare winter branches become clothed with fresh spring leaves, which continue to change through the summer and fall. Autumn color will not be spectacular, but it provides something further to be enjoyed. A trough planted entirely with perennial plants will look flat during the fall and winter months when these plants have gone dormant, and the permanent branch structure of little trees or shrubs will be appreciated. The same principles apply in selecting deciduous trees as with the evergreens.

What is the difference between a tree and a shrub? The textbooks tell us that a shrub is a perennial plant with many persistent woody stems arising from or near the base of the plant. A tree, on the other hand, has a single woody stem arising from the ground, with a single distinct trunk. In trough gardening, there is no need for this botanical distinction; as in other art forms, beauty is judged by the artist or designer, and all that matters is that the plant fits its role.

Finally, where a tree or shrub has a crucial role in your plan, select a true woody species rather than a perennial plant that looks like a woody shrub, for those plants may grow too fast. The true woody shrub retains its essential outline and form and will produce small amounts of new growth annually, but not enough to radically spoil the design. There is also nothing wrong with a little prudent trimming, when called for.

The list of deciduous trees and shrubs suitable for trough gardens is not very long. If the indicated annual growth rate is just a little too much, but a particular species is too appealing to reject, it is still worth trying, as the low fertility of the soil lessens and eventually slows growth. If the experiment fails there is always the option of removing the tree and trying something else.

The arctic birch, *Betula nana*, is good candidate. It has attractive tiny leaves with toothed margins. It is a bushy shrub with thin twigs, rather than the usual single-stemmed tree. It will accept a lean diet. Seek the tiniest clones that are listed. *B.* 'Trost's Dwarf' is most likely a dwarf variant of the common or white birch of Europe; it will grow to two or three feet tall, but very slowly. No one describes it better than Baldassare Mineo, owner of Siskiyou Rare Plant Nursery, in Oregon, where there is a lovely specimen: "...it is a slow-growing shrub with small, threadlike leaves and elegant habit that rivals and imitates the finest dissected-leaf forms of Japanese maple."

Sorbus reducta, from western China, is an appealing little thicket with tiny *Sorbus*-like leaves, composed of five to 15 toothed leaflets.

Little white flowers are carried in clusters, followed by pleasant pink fruit. Planted in a rock garden in fertile soil, it can make a suckering bush up 18 inches high; but it performs well under restricted conditions by remaining a low, stunted bush. Under these conditions the tiny leaves turn a bright red in the fall.

Ulmus parvifolia 'Hokkaido', Miniature Plant Kingdom, CA

The giant elm trees would not be expected to provide us with potential trough plants, but there is a race of tiny specimens originating from a species found in China, Japan and Korea: the Chinese elm, *Ulmus parvifolia*. *U. p.* 'Hokkaido' is one such dwarf form, and is popular with bonsai growers, owing to the small, neat leaves and nicely proportioned branches. This group of cultivars is naturally slow-growing, generating a well-shaped little tree which, with aging, attains a fissured and corky bark. Grown in a trough, it will not need the constant pruning or training of bonsai; once planted in the trough or sink garden, it can be left to grow naturally.

The mountains and circumpolar arctic regions offer many great plants for our small gardens, including little willows. They should be planted with caution: as with all willows, once they are established, there is a strong possibility that they will grow and take over. Upright, treelike cultivars are available and may be used, if excessive growth is continuously controlled by pruning and shaping.

Salix x *boydii* is the finest of the trough-sized willows. Although I risk provoking readers by describing a plant that is hard to find, I am reluctant to omit it entirely, fearing it could be overlooked, and that would be a tragedy. It is a natural hybrid between two or three Scottish species and found in the wild, during the 1880's, by William Boyd. He collected, rooted and distributed a few cuttings. Despite all efforts, this particular hybrid has never been found again. The young plants quickly take on a gnarled, aged appearance. The branches jut from the trunk in an angular manner, adding to the look of age. Dark green leaves, about half an inch or so, are orbicular (almost circular) in shape, with light-colored down on the undersides.

S. helvetica, a small, bushy, erect shrub, may be capable of slowly growing to three feet high (or less, depending upon the clone). But, with its attractive, small, gray-green, soft hairy leaves, it is well worth trying (and pruning) in a trough. *S. hastata* 'Wehrhahnni' may be just too large, but it is a delightful plant, with stout, reddish twigs and the most striking silvery catkins in spring.

Newsholme, in his new book on willows, lists that as one achieving six feet in height. Under *alpine specimens for rock gardens,* he suggests *S.* 'Hastata Lanata' (a cross between hastata and lanata) which only grows to two feet.

There is a wider selection of mat-forming willows, including both fast-growing varieties with long, slender, twiggy branches and contrasting varieties that make low, compact mats of short stems. *S. reticulata* is one of the most pleasing of the low willows, particularly in early spring when the plant is clothed in fresh, pale-green leaves covered with soft silky hairs. The hairs disappear as the leaves mature to dark green, with a conspicuous network of veining. Where a low woody carpet of branches is required, none can better this species.

A small willow with branches draping over the sides of sink garden is a sight that is hard to resist. Cultivars such as *S. repens* 'Boyd's Pendulous' or *S. repens* 'Iona' are both capable of performing this role. *S. repens* is a variable species with a wide distribution throughout the mountains of Europe. It is found with differing habits, from creeping, ground-hugging plants to erect, shrubby varieties. Early spring finds the twigs as well as the young leaves clothed in silky hair, the leaves maturing to dark green on their upper surfaces.

S. lapponicum is worth a try if it can be found. It is a small, tangled little shrub with hairy gray leaves.

S. x moorei is a hybrid that forms a spreading, bushy, twiggy mound about a foot tall and as much across. It sports small, shiny, dark green leaves with white undersides.

Rex Murfitt

Salix yezo-alpina is a fine willow for troughs, but needs a controlling hand. It is best in a trough of its own.

Joyce Fingerut

This trough at Ness Botanic Garden, England, offers
a perfect example of what the well-chosen plant in
the well-sited spot can achieve over time.

Chapter Five
Planting Plans for Troughs

Now it is time to pull together all you have learned about planting and siting garden troughs.

The sample plan shown in this chapter offers a number of troughs of differing plants and styles, each one tailored to suit a different environment, taste and level of gardening skill. There are suggestions for the setting of each trough, its plants, soil and mulch, as well as for the surrounding areas of companion plants. While we have assembled everything into one plan, you need not use it exactly as shown. Your own design can be limited to a single trough or one group. You may expand this plan for a larger area, or break it up to use in several different garden spots. The pavers can be of any material: slate, bluestone, sandstone or concrete. This particular plan has a pathway down the center, possibly leading to steps. It also incorporates an especially large paver to the left, designed to firmly support a chair from which to contemplate your creations.

The schematic drawing shows the pavers and troughs, and includes shaded areas surrounding the troughs to be left unpaved and available for companion plantings. The dimensions of the troughs are given, plus a sampling of paver sizes, in order to show the scale of the project and as an aid in ordering materials. Each trough, or group of troughs, is planted to suit a specific set of conditions: shady, sunny, moist, dry, etc. All plants listed for that trough have the same horticultural requirements, though they may come from different parts of the world. These plantings have been illustrated with ink drawings by Rex Murfitt. Plants that have been described in detail in Chapter Four are marked with an asterisk; the others receive a brief description here. The naming of the type of trough planting will in itself provide clues to the plants' needs: that is, a woodland trough requires moist shade and the drylands trough is suitable for sunny, dry conditions.

Probably, no single patio or garden will contain all of the growing conditions cited here, and no one gardener will be interested in all of the types of plants. So pick and choose, recombining troughs and plants to suit your preferences.

Above all, enjoy.

131

SAMPLE TROUGHS

SCHEMATIC DRAWING OF PATIO PLAN

LEFT SIDE

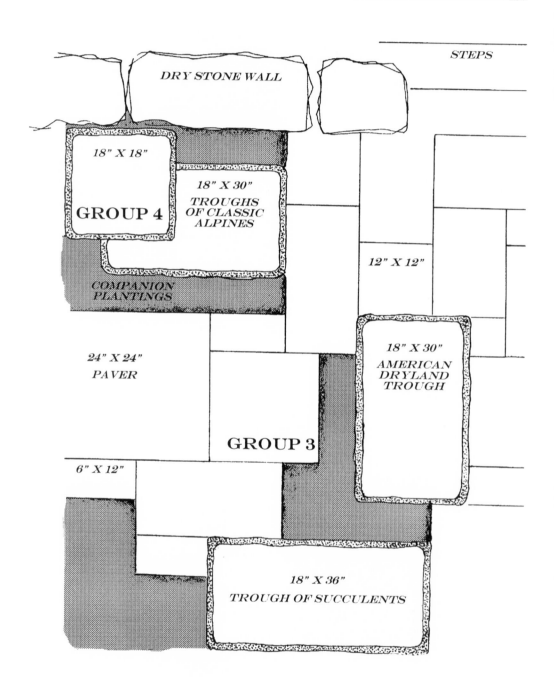

STEPS

DRY STONE WALL

18" X 18"

18" X 30"

TROUGHS OF CLASSIC ALPINES

GROUP 4

COMPANION PLANTINGS

12" X 12"

24" X 24" PAVER

18" X 30" AMERICAN DRYLAND TROUGH

GROUP 3

6" X 12"

18" X 36" TROUGH OF SUCCULENTS

SAMPLE TROUGHS

SCHEMATIC DRAWING OF PATIO PLAN

RIGHT SIDE

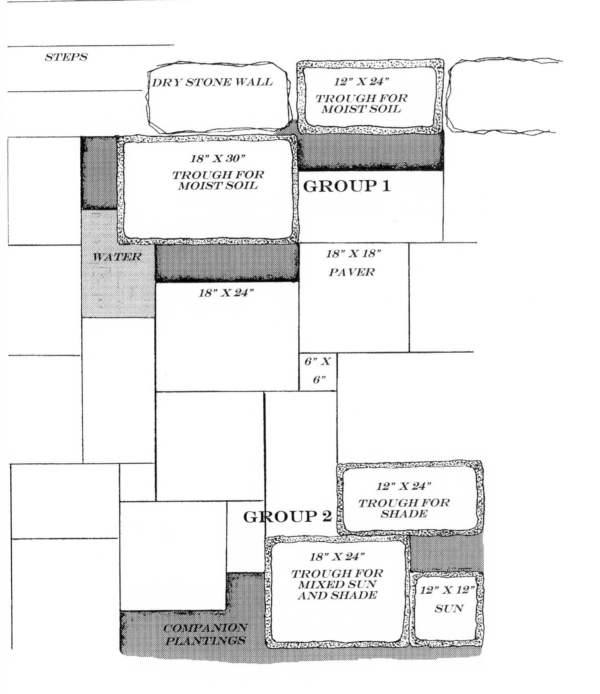

STEPS

DRY STONE WALL

12" X 24"
TROUGH FOR
MOIST SOIL

18" X 30"
TROUGH FOR
MOIST SOIL

GROUP 1

WATER

18" X 18"
PAVER

18" X 24"

6" X 6"

GROUP 2

12" X 24"
TROUGH FOR
SHADE

18" X 24"
TROUGH FOR
MIXED SUN
AND SHADE

12" X 12"
SUN

COMPANION
PLANTINGS

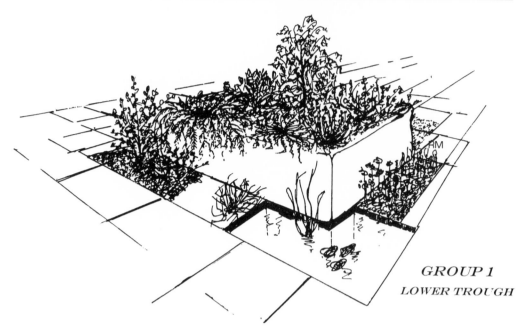

GROUP 1
LOWER TROUGH

Group 1. *Plants for Moist Conditions*

These two troughs and their companion plants are treated as a unit; the theme is plants for moist conditions. The soil for the troughs should be a rich organic mix that is moisture retentive, but note that the emphasis is upon keeping the plants cool rather than wet. A large component of humus, peat or anything organic should be present in the soil mix, but with sharp grit added for good drainage. Beware of too much fertility in the mix, or the plants will grow out of scale. Any rocks that are used should be of an acidic granite, not a limestone such as tufa. The mulch should be a scaled-down version of pine nuggets, or possibly coir—anything organic and of a fine texture.

The trough at the top right of the schematic drawing on the previous page should be embedded in a wall, serving as as the top course for a dry-laid stone wall. But it can also be perched on top of any kind of wall, or simply elevated on hypertufa legs or concrete blocks. It contains just one plant, a willow: *Salix yezo-alpina* (shown on page 129). This plant will grow well, perhaps too well for a short while, until the plant adjusts to the restrictions of a trough. The plant will need attentive pruning, possibly twice a season. But the strength and grace of its form and its lovely spring catkins will repay this work.

The full trough below it (pictured above) features mostly woody plants, with the herbaceous sorts being used as accessories; this is the reverse of the usual trough compositions. They all prefer a cool, moist position that is shaded, as a minimum, from the hottest afternoon sun. Suggested for this design are:

⟫ *Tsuga canadensis* (hemlock), offering a few cultivars that grow in proportions that fit nicely here: 'Jervis', 'Bennett's Minima' and 'Horsford'.

⟫ *Vaccinium* species, under the common names of, variously, blueberry, cranberry, etc, including a number of dwarf plants. Good compact

134

blueberry species are *V. moupinense* and *V. delavayi*, which is hardier. They grow only about a foot high and wide. *V. oxycoccus* 'Hamilton' is a creeping, congested form of cranberry with deep green, leathery, nearly stemless tiny disks for leaves.

⋙ *Empetrum nigrum*, the black crowberry. This species takes on a deep and somber winter coloring in its needle-like leaves. Its long, loose stems can grow to a foot in length, but lie gracefully about the ground, adding height only when they pile upon themselves.

⋙ *Ledum groenlandicum* 'Compactum', or *L. palustre diversipilosum* (which better tolerates warm climates). Both of these are small teaberries, members of the *Ericaceae*, the heath family. They sport crowded terminal clusters of flowers that are white, dreaming of pink.

⋙ *Betula nana.* If you prefer something deciduous in place of one of the evergreens, you might chose this very hardy little birch, whose charm lies mostly in its unexpected shrubby form, open and upright. At most, and only after some time, it will grow to about a meter high, but can be pruned.

Companion plants could include:

⋙ *Ophiopogon japonicus* 'Kyoto', or 'Kyoto Dwarf', a very dwarf grasslike lily. It can be grown in the trough, beside it in the ground, or in both places, to tie them together visually. The leaves are the thing, being rich black-green, tough, slightly curved and growing in tight tuffets. It can either be allowed to increase by its stolons and flow into the spaces open to it, or easily clipped back to a dark little hedgehog.

⋙ *Primula denticulata,* the popular drumstick primula. It will enjoy these moist conditions, and is available in a range of colors, including rose, pink, lavender and white. This plant normally grows to about 12 inches, but there is a dwarf variety available, now named *P. denticulata* 'Mini Form', which only grows to about six inches and has dark purple flowers. An effective design suggests itself, exploiting the contrasts in size.

⋙ *Equisetum hyemale.* This suggestion may send shudders through anyone who has grown or dealt with it in the garden. But, contained to an escape-proof pot, it adds a linear, reedy quality to a waterside planting. Because this plant tolerates wet conditions, the container can be without a drainage hole (for instance a cachepot), thus helping to hold "Houdini" within bounds.

Group 2. *Plants for Varied Sun and Shade*

The three troughs combined in this group vary in size and height. They center on an in-ground planting of a tree (not shown) with an upright form: possibly *Juniperus* 'Pencil Point', as an evergreen (actually everblue) exclamation mark. This site, which could be close to the side of a house, varies from shade to sun and therefore needs either a variety of plants, or plants adaptable to a variety of conditions.

The rear trough (next page, A) contains plants found in shaded gardens—the difference here is merely one of scale. The usual rocks can be replaced by a gracefully rotting tree branch or gnarled root in a fine state of decay. Plant suggestions for this trough include:

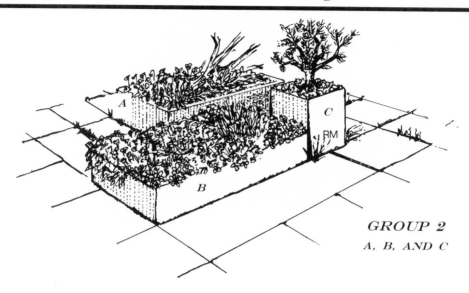

GROUP 2
A, B, AND C

⇢» The dwarf rhododendron, *R.* 'Yaku Fairy', the focus of the design. This could just as easily be *R. impeditum* (in a climate with cool summers), *R.* 'Kokensai', *R.* 'Mt. Seven Stars', *R.* 'Ginny Gee' or any of a number of excellent dwarf species and cultivars now available.

⇢» A choice plant for this site such as a *Soldanella* species, which features a rosette of deep green, nearly round leaves of some substance. Flower stalks will carry single, pendant, fringed lavender bells in early spring, if you are skilled or lucky. *S. montana* is the easiest species of this genus, but all are worth the effort.

⇢» *Hosta* 'Stefan Koya', providing dwarf shapely leaves and short stalks of summer flowers for almost no effort beyond the initial planting.

⇢» A slathering of moss for the finish, to fill all the crevices and climb over the trough sides. No more is needed to give an air of completeness, with restraint.

In the foremost trough (B), which lies mostly in the sun, the plants are allowed to create their own landscape. Dwarf species of flowering herbaceous perennials, roughly equal in height and growth patterns, but with differing flower colors and leaf textures, completely fill the planter. Their exuberant growth creates a froth and tumble of colors and shapes, rather like a miniature version of the best perennial borders. Little mulch will be needed, except at the outset, as the plants themselves cover every available inch. Any or all of these are suitable:

⇢» *Allium senescens glaucum*, a very refined onion with tufts of curved blue-gray leaves and a fall display of small globes of lavender florets.

⇢» *Aquilegia scopulorum.**

⇢» *Arabis blepharophylla*, a dwarf pink cress, blooming in earliest spring.

⇢» *Asperula gussonii*, with neat dark-green pads of fine foliage, smothered in spring with heads of small pink flowers.

⇛ *Dianthus* species.* Any dwarf dianthus will combine happily: *D. freynii, D. neglectus* or *D. simulans* (select the last option only if you live in the West; it simply doesn't flower well in the East).

⇛ *Geranium sessiliflorum* 'Nigricans', a dwarf hardy geranium whose value lies in its attractively different bronze foliage rather than its insignificant white flowers.

⇛ *Houstonia (Hedyotis) caerulea.* This species has variable common names: bluets, Quaker Ladies. By any name, it forms a soft bun of tiniest leaves, covered in the late spring by softly colored blue-gray flowers on wiry stems.

⇛ *Potentilla aurea.**

⇛ Saxifrages, especially of the encrusted or silver group, to provide additional contrast in foliage form and add arching plumes of color. *S. paniculata* 'Rosea' and *S. p.* 'Lutea' blend well together with their soft shades of red and yellow. Use *S.* 'Southside Seedling', whose white petals are so heavily spotted with copper that it is hard to be sure whether they are white or copper-colored. For a dash of pure silver, it is hard to beat some of the named hybrids, such as *S.* x *burnatii,* or *S.* 'Francis Cade', both with pure white, red-stemmed flower spikes.

Nearby, companion plants in the ground extend this idea, possibly using:

⇛ *Iris pumila,* a dwarf, occasionally reblooming iris, available in a myriad of colors to blend with any design.

⇛ *Globularia cordifolia* (or, equally easy-to-grow *G. meridionalis*), to clothe the ground with an evergreen mat of tiny, round, dark-green leaves, decorated with short-stemmed globes of light blue florets.

⇛ *Asarina procumbens,* offering everything that is soft: fuzzy leaves of a soft gray-green and snapdragon flowers of moonlight yellow, on reclining stems that soften the hard edges where the trough meets the ground.

The third trough in the group (C) is a deep one, at least as deep as wide, to contain a dwarf specimen, either a conifer, pruned in a spreading, bonsai manner or a deciduous tree, with an elegant winter branching pattern. Suggested are:

⇛ One of the upright dwarf pines, making an excellent statement when displayed in solitary splendor. A choicer Mugo variety would remain within scale for a while; or, where hardy, *Pinus sylvestris* 'Beuvronensis'.

⇛ *Ulmus parvifolia* 'Hokkaido', a miniature version of the stately elm. The leaves are deep green and completely in scale, while the trunk slowly accrues girth and dignity with the years.

Group 3. *Dryland and Succulent Plants for Full Sun*

The central trough duo in the schematic drawing, Group 3 contains plants that thrive under full sun. This is not to say that they will need no moisture whatsoever. But they are tough plants; they will do well, and offer beauty, with a minimum of attention. The growing medium needs to be very well drained,

GROUP 3

A

containing a major component of hard grits, fine pebbles or coarse sands. The pH should be neutral, even leaning towards slightly alkaline. The same grit or sand can be used as a top dressing; but neutral beige shades are preferable to glaring white, as a good deal of the mulch will be showing between plants in order to mimic a naturally sere habitat.

The back trough (A) features an assortment of American dryland plants, mostly from our western plains and mountains, such as:

⇒ *Lewisia cotyledon*. This is the showiest species of that genus, with succulent leaves varying in width from narrow to wide straps, arranged in a rosette that is attractive in itself. But this plant can also put on a non-stop flowering show for the whole of spring, the length of the show being matched by the breadth of its color range. The variable shades of pink of the straight species have been broadened (by careful breeding and selection) to include oranges, yellows and creams in the new cultivars.

⇒ *Petrophytum cinerascens*. The ultimate miniature spiraea, this is the easiest species of this genus to find, and to grow. The tiny leaves make a neat gray-green mound, which is topped by a cluster of white to cream flowers on a one- to two-inch stem.

⇒ *Eriogonum ovalifolium*, with the loveliest, lowest-growing mat of tiny oval (hence the name) white leaves. These are topped by short-stemmed buckwheat flowers varying in color from white through cream and yellow into shades of pink, rose and orange, all of which deepen with age, adding interest.

⇒ *Antennaria* species, the common pussytoes. Plants in this genus are easy to grow, but more difficult to contain. It is best to place your specimen in a corner, where it will prove invaluable, as it will do most of its spreading over the side of the trough.

138

⇨ *Cheilanthes* species: Yes, here are ferns for the sun! Plant *C. lanosa* for a hardy, gray, feathery-form plant. If you live in zone 7, or warmer, you can succeed with *C. argentea* (*Aleuritopteris argentea*). This is a stunning star (both in shape and in interest), with a startling white reverse to the palmate fronds—worth searching out under any name. These plants will appreciate a rock or two, to provide some cool relief to their roots.

The larger or more rambunctious plants that can be used in the ground around the base of the trough include:

⇨ *Festuca glauca* (sometimes still seen as *F. ovina glauca*), a fine-leaved, blue tufted grass. Regionally, there are several different dwarf cultivars, if you feel that the scale of the whole design calls for something smaller than the normal 18-inch height of the species.

⇨ *Yucca* species, in the same size category. The architectural stature of the hardy species, *Y. glauca*, in some settings, might overwhelm the composition. If you garden in a milder climate (perhaps zone 8) you might be able to grow one of the smaller species: *Y. baccata* or *Y. rupicola*, both Southwest natives.

⇨ *Penstemon hirsutus* 'Pygmaeus', right in scale, being a dwarf form of the straight species. Its nondescript, lightly hairy leaves are compensated by the four- to six-inch stalks of pale purple flowers. It will seed itself about, but with restraint.

⇨ Any sort of sempervivum or sedum. These do nicely here, while helping to tie the picture to the next trough, whose planting is composed almost entirely of succulent plants.

The second dryland trough (B, illustrated on the next page,) contains a richly textured planting of sedums and succulents; most of these are common, but a few are lesser known:

⇨ *Sedum spathulifolium.**

⇨ *Sedum dasyphyllum.**

⇨ *Delosperma*, a genus from South Africa that has turned out to be surprisingly hardy. Each species offers a different color in its daisy-like flower: *D. cooperi* (hardiest of the lot) will have a good-sized, silky magenta blossom; *D. nubigenum* blooms early and bright, in a brassy yellow; and *D. ashtonii* arrives more subtly, in pink. Best for a small or crowded trough is *D. aberdeenense*, with small (half-inch) purple flowers. All should be hardy to zone 7, perhaps 6, with protection.

⇨ *Talinum calycinum*, with leaves like narrow cylinders, clustered into a tuft. The portulaca-like flowers dancing at the ends of four-inch wiry stems are small but vivid, in red or purple.

⇨ *Orostachys furusei* and *O. iwarenge*, which have a rosette form much like a large sempervivum. The startling difference is in the coloring, which is a ghostly gray, shading into pink. It can be used as a very effective contrast.

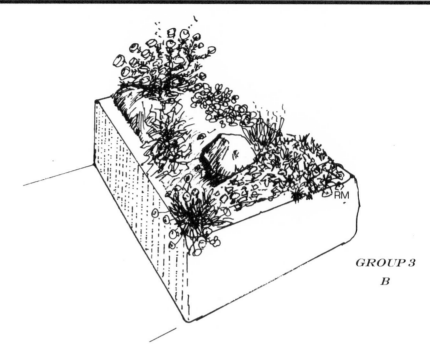

GROUP 3
B

⇛ *Aethionema* 'Warley Rose', with its gray needle-like foliage draping down the side, adding a feeling of age to the planting. When the bright pink flowers appear in the early summer, it is often mistaken for a daphne.

⇛ *Ephedra minima*, or *Carmichaelia enysii* in warmer climates (at least zone 7), both offering a shrubby, but leafless, form. They add a different sort of texture and substance to a planting, plus a year-round green presence.

Group 4. *Classic Alpines*

Mounting the smaller of the two troughs on top of the larger is a novel way of achieving variety in presentation; it adds a design element that can be used in several situations, perhaps where space is at a premium. This arrangement also lends itself to a high alpine planting scheme, where the smaller species can be enjoyed from a higher viewpoint.

The soil mixture may consist of one part topsoil, one part peatmoss and leafmold mixed together, with the remaining part a mixture of coarse sand and grit. The plants will require some protection from the hot sun during summer months, plus precautions to ensure that the soil does not dry out for long periods.

Using alpine plants provides an opportunity to feature some substantial rock work and to build a small rock garden within the trough, complete with crevices and miniature cliffs. Tufa rock or some of the pumice stones are excellent for this work, as they are usually soft and somewhat porous, with a pleasant color. Limestone, especially if it is attractively contoured and has lots of rugged character, is also suitable. The plants recommended for this scheme will have no aversion to the limestone.

The complementary top dressing should be of stone chips or gravel, taking care that a generous dressing is worked under the foliage, up to and around the

GROUP 4

crown of each plant, with at least an inch of cover over the entire soil surface. This gravel mulch looks more natural if it is of the same color as the rocks in the trough. Lacking a convenient source, take a heavy hammer to the leftover stone and make your own top dressing.

This situation might be the right place for one of the more treelike forms of dwarf spruce, where its upright character will accentuate the miniature cliffs and gorges. Choose *Picea abies* 'Bennett's Miniature' or *P. omorika* 'Gnom' for a slightly more irregular outline.

This planting plan enables the use of all those fascinating hard cushion plants, the lovely little saxifrages, as well as a few of the silver saxifrages. For the rock crevices:

➤➤ *Draba rigida** or *D. polytricha.**

➤➤ The little cushion saxifrages with their range of flower colors. They offer choices of pink, yellow or white. *S.* 'Cranborne' is always a favorite, with pink flowers and a silver mound of foliage. For a change of color, there are several yellows to choose from, with mats of foliage in either gray-green or bright green. *S.* 'Boston Spa' is an accommodating hybrid with dark green spiky foliage and three-inch flower stems carrying three to four primrose-yellow flowers. *S.* x *paulinae*, with its tufted, gray-green rosettes has yellow flowers on short stems. *S. burseriana* 'Gloria' has large glistening white flowers on red stems borne over a carpet of silvery foliage. For variety, a few of the silver saxifrages could be incorporated, but in the interest of space, select the smaller varieties. One that never fails to draw attention is *S. cochlearis* 'Minor' with its tight silver rosettes and plentiful supply of white flowers.

⇛ As an alternative to featuring saxifrages there are other alpines that offer a different plan. Use, for example, the alpine primulas; or choose some of the other cushion plants described in Chapter Four.

Companion plantings can be composed of all those plants that you love but are too big for the trough. Carpet the ground with *Phlox subulata* or *P. douglasii*, colorful armerias or the larger *Dianthus* species. Campanulas and saponarias are useful for extending the period of peak flowering.

DISPLAYING THE FINISHED TROUGH GARDEN

Trough gardens are often shown mounted on supports or low pedestals, a popular treatment among trough gardeners. The practice seems to have originated from the earliest exponents of the art, who believed that it enabled easier management and viewing of the plants if the trough was raised from the ground. Attractive blocks of the same stone as the trough were preferred, using two pieces at each end, rather than one single piece in the center. Stability is the paramount consideration: no one wants a trough to fall on a foot while replanting or weeding.

There are no set rules regarding how many inches the trough should be raised; it is more a matter of scale and personal taste. It will soon become apparent when it is too high: the arrangement will look unbalanced and insecure. Six inches is about right for a trough measuring 18 by 24 inches by six or eight inches deep. The more substantial the bases, the higher it is possible to raise the garden—even as much as 12 inches. Experiment with the height and type of base, preferably while the trough is empty.

The horticultural considerations in raising a trough or allowing it to remain in contact with the ground are also matters of opinion. A raised trough will have no problem with drainage, as there is nothing to hinder excess water passing through the drainage holes, whereas one in contact with the soil could easily develop a drainage problem, particularly if worms and other forms of soil life are active. On the other hand, where moisture retention is desirable, there will be some benefit from contact with the ground. However, this issue will not influence the success or failure of a planting by very much. The climate, suitable choice of plants, depth and type of soil, and amount of shade or sun will be the key.

Rex Murfitt

Sources and Resources

Over the years, in gardening, home decor and landscaping journals, there have been many, many articles about making hypertufa troughs. We hope with this book to integrate this information into one comprehensive source.

The North American Rock Garden Society's *Handbook on Troughs*, printed in 1996, is a fine introductory booklet. It covers trough-making as well as trough-planting. To obtain a copy, send a check for $6.00, payable to NARGS, to: **NARGS, PO Box 67, Millwood, NY, 10546.**

In this section we supply our best sources of information and goods, starting with plant resources and ending with cement and trough construction resources. We include texts that were used directly in the writing of this book as well as the best of those references that have contributed to our general horticultural educations.

ROCK AND ALPINE GARDENING
Books, General

❖ *A Rock Garden in the South*. Elizabeth Lawrence. Existing and forthcoming editions.

❖ *Alpines*. Will Ingwersen. Sagapress, Inc./Timber Press, Inc., Portland, OR, 1991.

❖ *Collectors' Alpines: Their Cultivation in Frames and Alpine Houses.* Royton E. Heath. Collingridge Books, England, 1964.

❖ *Encyclopedia of Alpines*. 2 volumes. The Alpine Garden Society, Woking, 1994.

❖ *Index of Garden Plants:* The New RHS Dictionary. Mark Griffiths Timber Press, Portland, OR, 1994.

❖ *Manual of Alpine Plants*. Will Ingwersen. Ingwersen & Dunnsprint Ltd., England, 1978.

❖ *Miniature Gardens*. Anne Ashberry. C. Arthur Pearson, Ltd., London, 1951.

❖ *Miniature Rock Gardening in Troughs and Pans* (Later re-issued as *Rock Plants for Small Gardens*). Royton E. Heath. W.H. & L. Collingridge Ltd., London, 1957.

❧ *Pleasures and Problems of a Rock Garden.* Louise Beebe Wilder. Doubleday, Doran & Co., Garden City, NY, 1932

❧ *Rock Garden Plants.* Clarence Elliott. Edward Arnold, 1936.

❧ *Rock Garden Plants of North America*: an anthology from the Bulletin of the North American Rock Garden Society. Timber Press in association with NARGS. Portland, OR, 1996.

❧ *Rock Gardening.* H. Lincoln Foster. Houghton Mifflin Company, Boston, MA, 1968.

❧ *Rocky Mountain Alpines.* Rocky Mountain chapter, American Rock Garden Society (now North American Rock Garden Society). Timber Press, Portland, OR, 1986.

Books, Special Genera

❧ *Androsaces.* G. F. Smith and D. B. Lowe. The Alpine Garden Society, Woking, 1977

❧ Campanulas. Peter Lewis and Margaret Lynch. Published in association with the Hardy Plant Society. Christopher Helm, London, England, Timber Press, Portland, OR, 1989.

❧ *Campanulas—Their Cultivation and Classification.* H. Clifford Crook. Country Life Limited, Charles Scribner's Sons, 1951.

❧ *Conifers—the Illustrated Encyclopedia.* D. M. Van Gelderen and J. R. P. Van Hooey Smith. Royal Boskoop. Horticultural Society/Timber Press, Portland, OR, 1996.

❧ *The Dianthus.* Will Ingwersen. England. 1949.

❧ *Dwarf Bulbs.* Brian Mathew. Arco Publishing Company, Inc., NY, 1973.

❧ *Dwarf Rhododendrons.* Peter A. Cox, in Association with The Royal Horticultural Society, England. Macmillan Publishing Co., Inc., NY, 1973.

❧ *Flowers of Greece and the Balkans.* Oxford University Press, 1980.

❧ *Gentians.* David Wilkie. Country Life Limited, Charles Scribner's Sons, NY, 1936.

❧ *The Genus Gentiana.* Josef J. Halda. Sen, Dobre, CZ 1996.

✤ *The Genus Lewisia*. Brian Mathew. The Royal Botanic Gardens, Kew, in association with Christopher Helm and Timber Press, Portland, OR, 1989.

✤ *The Genus Phlox*. Edgar T. Wherry. Morris Arboretum of the University of Pennsylvania, Philadelphia, PA, 1955.

✤ *Handbook of Cultivated Sedums*. Ronald L. Evans. Science Reviews Limited, England, 1983.

✤ *Hilliers' Manual of Trees & Shrubs. H. G. Hillier. David & Charles, England, 1975.*

✤ *The Iris*. Brian Mathew. Universe Books, NY, 1981.

✤ *Manual of Cultivated Conifers*. Gerd Krussman. Timber Press, Portland, OR, 1985.

✤ *Manual of Dwarf Conifers*. H. J. Welch. Charles T. Branford, Newton, MA 1979.

✤ *A Manual of Saxifrages and their Cultivation*. D.A. Webb and R.J. Gornall. Timber Press, Portland, OR, 1989.

✤ *Porophyllum Saxifrages*. Horny, Webb, Byam. Grounds. Stamford, 1986.

✤ *Primula*. John Richards. Timber Press, Portland, OR, 1993.

✤ *Sempervivum*. R. Lloyd Praeger. RHS, London, 1932.

✤ *Willows—The Genus Salix*. Christopher Newsholme. Timber Press, Portland, OR, 1992.

Plant Societies

The very best sources of information on plants for your troughs are the various rock and alpine garden societies. There are many around the world; and each, in turn, has many regional and local chapters.

In North America, the **North American Rock Garden Society (NARGS)** operates at two levels - both open to membership, each with unique offerings. The National sponsors an annual Seed Exchange, with a listing of over 6,000 taxa donated by over 600 members, gathered from gardens and the wild, worldwide. The NARGS Quarterly carries articles on plants of interest, whether they originate in the mountains, plains, woodlands or gardens, and advice (based upon experience) on growing them. The whole is well illustrated by expert color photographs. Three annual national meetings unite the members, offering them an opportunity to hear world and local authorities, and to visit private gardens or choice plant sites in the mountains.

145

✤ To join this exceptional organization, write to: Membership Secretary PO Box 67 Millwood, New York 10546 e-mail: mommens@ibm.net

When you contact the Membership Secretary, be sure to ask about the local chapter nearest you: there are well over 30 chapters in the United States (including Alaska) and Canada. Local meetings include speakers, plant sales, field trips and garden visits, as well as the immediacy of knowing your gardening neighbors.

✤ More information may be viewed at their website: www.nargs.org

In the U.K., there are two such excellent organizations: **The Alpine Garden Society** and the **Scottish Rock Garden Club**. Both have very high caliber Seed Exchanges and outstanding publications: the AGS's *Quarterly Bulletin* and the SRGC's twice yearly Journal, *The Rock Garden*. Again, each organization has its several local chapters; inquire about these when you apply for membership:

✤ **Alpine Garden Society**, The Secretary, AGS Centre, Avon Bank, Pershore, Worcestershire WR10 3JP U.K.

✤ **The Scottish Rock Garden Club,** Mrs. J. Thomlinson, Membership Secretary, 1 Hillcrest Road, Bearsden, Glasgow G61 2EB Scotland, U.K.

Farther afield, there are other international organizations well worth joining for their publications and seed exchanges even if you will never attend a single meeting:

✤ **The New Zealand Alpine Garden Society** PO Box 2984, Christchurch, New Zealand.

✤ **The Rock Garden Club of Prague** offers their quarterly bulletin, *Skalnicky,* with accompanying English abstracts; the Seed List is, of course, in botanically correct Latin. Write to **Klub Skalnickaru,** Praha, Marikova 5, 162 00 Praha 6, Czech Republic.

All of the above organizations will give you further access to the exciting world of rock and alpine gardening: worldwide travel, shares in seed collecting expeditions, conferences, specialty plant societies, acquisitions of rare plants and books.

Alpine-L, the Electronic Rock Garden Society. Alpine-L is an electronic mailing list on rock gardening and dwarf and alpine plants, including their botany (There is even a list Taxonomist, to settle questions and quibbles). Discussions and articles on this and related subjects constitute the major scope of the List, which welcomes both beginners and experts. The List is monitored; all messages are subject to approval by the listowners.

✣ To become a member of Alpine-L, you must send, via e-mail, a SUBSCRIBE command to the following address:

Listserv@nic.surfnet.NL

✣ The command must appear in the body of the email, all on one line, in the following format: subscribe alpine-l Your Name, City & State or Jurisdiction Hardiness Zone Rockgarden Club (if appropriate). For example: subscribe alpine-l Reginald Farrer, Washington DC Z7 NARGS

✣ If you have any questions or need help in any way, write to the active listowners (Harry Dewey and Louise Parsons) at:

Alpine-L-Request@nic.surfnet.NL

Sources of Plants and Seeds

The nurseries and seedhouses listed below need no hyperbole; we have found them to be reliable to deal with, offering uniformly fine products. Many will require a fee for their catalog—do not begrudge it. Aside from the fact that printing and mailing costs are soaring, a good catalog is a useful reference work, whether or not you buy the plants or seeds. These are but a few of the many fine suppliers of suitable plants and seeds.

Plants

✣ **Forestfarm**
Ray and Peg Prag
990 Tetherow Road
Williams, OR 97544-9599
An unusually large number of plants offered, both woody and herbaceous; many difficult to find elsewhere.

✣ **Heronswood Nursery**
Dan Hinckley
7530 288th Street
NE Kingston, WA 98346
Rare plants and new introductions from the plant-explorer owner.

❖ **Miniature Plant Kingdom**
Don Herzog
4125 Harrison Grade Road
Sebastopol, CA 95472
Dwarfest forms of a wide variety of plants, woody and herbaceous, alpine and lowland.

❖ **Mt. Tahoma Nursery**
Rick Lupp
28111-112 Avenue E
Graham, WA 98338
An emphasis on alpine plants, with a minor in dwarf conifers.

❖ **Siskyou Rare Plant Nursery**
Baldassare Mineo
2825 Cummings Road Medford, OR 97501
Alpine and other dwarf plants, as well as full-size perennials.

Seeds

❖ **Alplains Seeds and Plants**
Alan Bradshaw
32315 Pine Crest Court
Kiowa, CO 80117
Wild-collected seed of native American plants from western mountains and plains.

❖ **Jim and Jenny Archibald**
"Bryn Collen"
Ffostrasol, Llandysul
Dyfed, SA44 5SB
Wales, U.K.
Wild-collected seeds from the mountains of Europe and America, as well as their own extensive garden.

❖ **Karmic Exotix Nursery**
Andrew Osyany
Box 146
Shelburne, Ontario
L0N 1S0 Canada
Seeds from several Eastern Europe collectors, of plants native to the mountains of Turkey, Greece, and Central Asia.

❖ **Northwest Native Seeds**
Ron Ratko
2342 N. Main Street, Apartment L
Salinas, CA 93906
Wild-collected seed, with very specific information regarding site and plant description.

CONSTRUCTION TECHNIQUES AND SUPPLIES
Working with Cement and Hypertufa

Books

❖ *Basic Construction Techniques.* Bureau of Naval Personnel. Dover Publications, Inc., NY, 1972.

❖ *Design and Control of Concrete Mixtures, Thirteenth Edition (rev.).* Steven H. Kosmatka and William C. Panarese. Portland Cement Association, Skokie, IL, 1994.

❖ *Engineering Materials: Properties and Selection.* Kenneth G. Budinski. Prentice Hall, NJ, 1996.

❖ *Properties of Concrete*, Fourth and Final Edition. A. M. Nevill. John Wiley and Sons, NY, 1996. (Highly recommended.)

Websites

❖ **Portland Cement Association:** www.portcement.org

❖ **American Society for Testing Materials:** www.astm.org   email: service@local.astm.org

Artist and Lecturer

❖ **Roberta Berg**, artist and gardener, has found hypertufa to be an excellent medium for personal artistic expression in the garden (see pages 43, 47, and 48). She has used this material in innovative and creative ways for ornaments and accessories. She shares her ideas and expertise in lectures and demonstrations. Contact her at 60 Cedar Street, Wenham, MA, 01984.

CONSTRUCTION PRODUCTS

Reinforcement Fibers

❖ **Nycon, Inc.** (nylon), 101 Cross Street Westerly, RI 02891-2407.
401-596-3955 800-456-9266
www.nycon.com   nycon@aol.com

❖ **Hi-Tech Fibers, Inc.** (polypropylene), 306 Main Street, Edgefield, SC
29824.
www.secnet.com/prods/div3/03240.html

❖ **Fibermesh** (polypropylene), Synthetic Industries, 4019 Industry Drive,
Chattanooga, TN 37416.   423-892-7243
www.fibermesh.com   Email: fibermesh@aol.com

Cement Colors, Dry

❖ **True Tone by Davis Colors**,

7101 Muirkirk Road	3700 East Olympic Boulevard
Beltsville, MD 20705	Los Angeles, CA 90023
301-210-3400	213-269-7311
www.daviscolors.com	1-800-800-6856

Cement Colors, Liquid

❖ **Aqua-Sperse, Mortar Majic Co.**, Box 173, Bridgeport, PA 19405.

Concrete Stains

❖ **L. M. Scofield Company**

6533 Bandini Boulevard	4155 Scofield Road,
Los Angeles, CA 90040	Douglasville, GA 30134
213-720-3000	770-920-6000
1-800-800-9900	

Liquid Acrylic

❖ **Embond, Emerson Resources**, 600 Markley Street Norristown, PA
19401.   610-279-7450

❖ **Acryl 60, Thoro System Products**, 7800 N.W. 38Th Street, Miami, FL
33166-6599.

Index of Plants

* Refers to photograph or illustration.

151

General Index

* Refers to photograph or illustration.
See also *Index of Plants*, page 151.

159

creating and planting garden troughs

About the Authors

Joyce Fingerut

A Philadelphia native, Joyce Fingerut's horticultural career follows her first degree and career in psychology research and data analysis. She is also a graduate of the program at the Arboretum of the Barnes Foundation, Merion, Pennsylvania, and has taken additional coursework in Landscape Design and Construction at Delaware Valley College of Science and Agriculture and at Longwood Gardens. She recently edited *The Trough Handbook* for the North American Rock Garden Society.

She has designed and built award-winning exhibits for the Philadelphia Flower Show from 1980 to 1996, with emphasis on rock garden plants and alpine troughs. She gives lectures and workshops in various aspects of trough making and horticulture for organizations and arboreta throughout eastern North America.

Currently, Joyce Fingerut is National Vice-President for the North American Rock Garden Society, and is slated to become its next President. She also organizes its international Speakers' Tour Project.

Rex Murfitt

Born in England, Rex Murfitt trained as a nurseryman, later specializing in alpine plants at the famous W. E. Th. Ingwersen, Birch Farm Hardy Plant Nursery at Gravetye, Sussex. There, he trained under Walter Ingwersen VMH and his son Will Ingwersen VMH, who taught him the art of propagation and cultivation of alpine plants. He traveled widely with Will Ingwersen, building rock gardens for clients. From these great gardeners he learned the romance and lore of alpine plants.

Later he worked in large English gardens including J. Spedan Lewis's gardens at Longstock Park in Hampshire, caring for the greenhouses and orchid collection, as well as a growing alpine collection. Eventually he became Head Gardener to Mrs. Constance Spry at Winkfield Place, near Windsor, where plants were grown for her famous flower arrangements. He helped develop her white garden, based on the one at Sissinghurst Castle. Under the guidance of Graham Stuart Thomas, he undertook the care of a large collection of old fashioned roses.

He later moved to New York, and with Frank and Anne Cabot, started Stonecrop Nurseries Inc., at Cold Spring On Hudson, an alpine nursery based on English traditional methods. Stonecrop displayed rock gardens at Flower Shows in New York City and Philadelphia.

Rex Murfitt now grows alpines for pleasure at home in Victoria, B.C., Canada. His particular interests include collecting saxifrages, and he has a growing love for North American alpines. When not in the garden, he devotes time to photographing alpine plants and recording the efforts of the distinguished alpine gardeners he was fortunate enough to have known. He frequently prepares lectures and writes articles on alpine gardening.

Jane Grushow